NINE DECADES:

HOW I LIVED THEM

D1617261

NINE DECADES:

HOW I LIVED THEM

WILLIAM GREENE

My heartfelt thanks to those, who helped in so many different ways to make my "last hurrah" a pleasant experience: the Bren and Campbell families, Jeanne Fancher, Everett and Doris Fourre, Linda Manley, Kiley Masterson, Brenda De River, Wendy Scheibel, Evelyn Scott, Mary Stough, the Vaughn family, and Keith and George Yeager.

Copyright ©1991 William Greene

First American Printing

All rights reserved. No part of this book may be reproduced in any form or by any electronic or mechanical means including information storage and retrieval systems without permission in writing from   the publisher, except by a reviewer.

Library of Congress Catalog Card Number:
90-52853

ISBN: 0-934257-47-7

Book design by Lysa McDowell

Published by Story Press, Inc.
d.b.a. Story Line Press
Three Oaks Farm
Brownsville, OR
97327-9718

CONCORDIA UNIVERSITY LIBRARY
PORTLAND OR 97211

TO MY SISTER ANNE

for dedicating her life to the welfare of retarded children

INTRODUCTION
MEET MY FRIEND WILLIAM

By Gary Todd Campbell
Lacey, Washington—1991

My friend and neighbor, William M. Greene, was born in a Russian ghetto during the turbulent last decades of the nineteenth century, and lived through the traumatic events that brought about the final collapse of both czarism and capitalism in 1917. He was one of the seven children—six sons and a daughter—who survived the fourteen born to a Jewish family named Greenstein.

I learned a great deal about my friend William—his childhood in Russia's violent anti-Semitic environment, his low opinion of those whose decisions and lifestyles are based on tradition, the role of his brothers in early Zionism and socialism, his family's exodus from Russia, and his sad discovery that the streets of Canada and the United States are not paved with gold.

I talked with him for the first time in the summer of 1980, a day or two after he and his little cocoa-colored dog Willy became next-door neighbors. I was by the fence that separates our homes and saw him wrestling with some unpacked cartons on the patio, some 50 feet from me.

"Can I do anything to help you?" I shouted. He raised his head, studied me for a moment, and replied: "Yes, you can help me find a wife, a young one.

My six former wives were all young, and I don't see why I should change now."

I was amazed at what I found in the five-room home of this poor, nondescript, sad-looking old man. There were enough books piled on the floor in front of bookcases to supply a small library. There were encyclopedias, dictionaries in several languages, copies of paintings by Chagal, Rembrandt and Daumier, a fifty year old Underwood typewriter, records, tapes and manuscripts.

He seemed a perfect subject for one of those stories in Reader's Digest titled "The Most Unforgettable Character I Ever met," but it soon became clear that what he had to say, and deeply believed in, would never fit their "power of positive thinking" style.

I asked him why he had such a dislike for tradition—mainstream America, I said, would collapse without it, and Tevye the milkman in FIDDLER ON THE ROOF opened with a song about tradition. "What's wrong with it?"

And he said: "Life is a dynamic process and tradition shackles it. You can see it everywhere today. Technology has changed the world, but those who always controlled the world still control it. The "pursuit of happiness," promised everyone in the Declaration of Independence, remains a traditional lottery, and even here those who can afford ten tickets have an advantage. "Tradition, tradition," sang Tevye the milkman—with God's help we're still starving."

William's enlightenment began with the Old Testament in Russia when he was eight years old. As the youngest male in the family, he was required, by Hebrew tradition, to start the observance of the annual Passover, which symbolizes the plight of enslaved Jews in Egypt, with a Hebrew question to his father:

"Ma nishtano heleile hazeh mikol haleilem?" (Why is this night different from other nights?)

His father replied that on this night we recall the suffering and bitterness experienced by our ancestors, and then pointed to bits of horseradish and hard-boiled eggs floating in heavily-salted water on the table. They are symbols of their suffering. Then his father began to read the story as written in Exodus in the Old Testament.

This was, of course, not his first Passover. But this time it was different. This time he didn't just sit there waiting for the ritual to end, and his mother to start the important part—bringing in the lavish dinner that always began with chicken soup and matzo balls. This time he listened carefully, because it was he who gave the signal for his father to start relating the great drama called Exodus.

The traumatic event that converted him into a non-traditionalist came when his father began to enumerate the plagues God heaped on the innocent Egyptians because their Pharaoh turned a deaf ear when Moses pleaded: "Let my people go."

It was a part of the Passover ritual. Nothing new; his mother always placed before each of them a goblet filled with wine made from cherries for the occasion, and each time his father named a plague they dropped a little of the wine into a copper container on the floor.

His mind was whirling and his hand shook as he clutched the goblet. It was dreadful. Each time God created a plague the Pharaoh "hardened his heart" and said: "No." First God turned all the water into blood, then covered the land with frogs, gnats, flies, a pestilence, body boils, hail, darkness, finally he ordered the oldest innocent son of every Egyptian family killed. Why didn't God simply snap his fingers and just kill the Pharaoh? My friend William never forget that Passover and the six Hebrew words, with which he opened it.

"I think," said William, "the X-rated stuff should be cut out of the Old Testament before children read it." I said "amen."

But what intrigued me most was the nontraditional way he educated himself, his hunger for knowledge.

Near the end of the nineteen twenties, he told me, he managed, by what he called a "fluke," to break away from his job as a laborer and machinist helper in a railroad roundhouse to become—of all things— a journalist.

He had by that time lived in America for eighteen years—twelve in Canada and six in the United States, and on the principle that necessity is the mother of invention, he began the struggle to survive by collecting knowledge from whatever source was available.

His schooling at that time, he said, was a "yes and a no." Several months after arriving in Canada he had to enroll at a public school and in a class for "greenhorns" (immigrants) to learn English. Before the end of the first week he discovered that instructors in Canada were not different from those in Russia— they were no good.

In Russia seven years earlier, he was viciously punished by an evil- smelling "melamed" (teacher) for being out of tune with the rest of the young boys song-singing the "Aleph-Beth-Gimel-Daleth" (A-B-C-D)— the opening letters of the Hebrew alphabet.

In Canada, he found himself in a line of fellow "greenhorns" before a teacher who spoke three languages and wanted to know how much English they had already absorbed, and let her hear how they pronounced the words.

Well, he had heard many words and phrases in the months before he enrolled, but the meaning of a lot of them he did not yet know. So he picked one for her to hear that contained the word "Jew." When his turn came, he took a deep breath and said loudly and clearly "Oi vey; fucking Jew." He was sent to the principal, who ordered him to hold out his hands palms outward and seemed to experience a thrill each time he blasted them with the end of a barber's shaving strap. William told me that as he watched the tight-lipped principal administering punishment and seeming to enjoy it, he could not help but recall the evil-smelling "melamed" and God's plagues on Egypt.

Then, he said, he could see the Irish kid—from whom he heard the words—with his brogans and knickers as he stood about ten feet from him waiting for a streetcar. "Hullo," I said. "Take a powder Sheeny," he replied. He hadn't yet heard the derisive anti-Semitic words "kike" and "sheeny" and thought the Irish kid was talking about a "machina," the Russian word for machine, so he said again, "Yes, hullo. The Irish kid gave me a contemptuous look, spit into an imaginary spittoon, and said: Go away, fucking Jew."

That was when William decided he could do a better job educating himself than a school could. He continued turning up at school, he told me, not to become educated, but mostly because as a European immigrant he feared the authorities—including his parents—a fear that remained for years.

As a matter of fact, the school tests that he often

passed came from what he learned away from school.

He began the task of learning to read with the help of books that printed Yiddish on the left pages and their translations into English on the right side. And, as they say today—he never left home without a primer in his pocket.

He was not interested, he said, in how the words were pronounced or what they were called in grammar. All he wanted to know was what the English words meant, in order to avoid more "fucking Jew" fiascoes.

It was not until radio became available in thousands of homes in both Canada and the United States that he learned how to pronounce infrequently heard words. He learned that the "ch" in "melancholy" is pronounced as a "k". "Plague" and "intrigue" are pronounced without sounding the "ue". A "fish fillet" is a "fish fillay" and "naive" is pronounced "na-eeve".

Uniquely, it was his dialect, created by mispronounced English words with doses of Russian and Yiddish words, which made it possible for him— years before radio appeared—to make friends and influence pretty young women. "You speak cha-mingly," said an 18 year old brunette, squeezing herself closer to him.

When he had accumulated a sufficient vocabulary he began to become more and more interested in what he was reading. He made a wonderful discovery—the children's departments in libraries.

He learned that astronomy began with man's interest in astrology and, chemistry in alchemy, how man discovered fire and how man learned to separate iron from ore. From then on, you might say, it was "all systems go." He spent every minute he could spare, wherever he was, whatever he was doing to earn a livelihood, in libraries.

Near the end of the twenties, he was able to boast that his way of becoming self-educated had been vindicated by none other than the English novelist H. G. Wells. In his book about two children named Joan and Peter, Wells insisted that the function of instructors should not be to inform students, but to teach them how to become informed. In this way they will not only remember better and longer what they have learned, but in the process of learning they will also be exposed to a great deal of other important information.

William's own search for knowledge expanded in that manner. A quote in a magazine by H. L. Mencken intrigued him, and he visited the library for information about this writer. Overhearing the words "electoral college" by fellow railroad workers was the catalyst for his interest in the United States Constitution. A report of a train accident caused by a malfunctioning magnet in a trackside pole signal got him interested in physics.

In the fall of 1928 my friend William became a member of the Fourth Estate, a name given the press in 1790 by Edmund Burke, a member of the English parliament. Referring to the three estates that dominated nations in those days—the nobility, clergy and the commons—he pointed a finger to the reporters' gallery, and said: "There is the Fourth Estate which is more important than all." Today Congress points to itself with pride and views with alarm the independent members of the Fourth Estate.

It was some time before William adjusted to his new strange environment. He had never seen a tele-

type machine, nor had he ever had as fellow workers college-trained people. But with encouragement
from his unusual editor, and even more unusual publisher,
he was soon off like a race horse.

His very first assignment set the pattern for his
writing for newspapers and radio, but only when
he had a free hand to write. And when he did have
a free hand, he added something to the subject, ranging
from an entertaining anecdote to the 23rd Psalm.
He discovered that it is possible to discuss important issues in an interesting and entertaining manner, without in any way diminishing the subject's
importance. "You want to hear a funny story? There
was this Jewish rabbi, Protestant bishop and Catholic priest who found it necessary to cross a narrow
river. Both the Jewish rabbi and Protestant bishop
made it, but were soaked to above their knees.

The Catholic priest hopped across without any trouble.
"How did you do it, Father?" "I did it," said the
priest, "the way Jesus did. He knew where the rocks
in the river were."

The editor had asked him to write a short story
for the feature page of the paper about a new movie
house that was being built a few blocks from their
office. What he added was a comment about the bricks
that were being laid to create the walls. "By the way,"
he wrote, "there is something interesting about the
bricks. To all of us they are just a bunch of solid
objects, but to those who know something about Albert
Einstein's theory of ' relativity', each brick is made
up of millions upon millions of atoms, each of which
contains protons and electrons that work against each
other and make the countless millions of atoms in-
finitesimal worlds whirling in space." His very first

article, he told me, won an award. The theater manager gave him a free pass for the theater's opening night.

Einstein himself, he said, explained his relativity theory to a pretty young school student this way: Time is relative, he told her, because if she sat for half an hour on her sweetheart's lap, time would pass without her even being aware of it. But it would not be the same if she sat on the top of a hot stove.

Working for a newspaper was an opportunity of a lifetime, and my friend William latched onto it like a dog to a juicy bone. As a reporter he now had access to people in every walk of life. He was now able to confirm his conclusions he reached during the last eighteen years, alter them or expand them, or even abandon them. He had, for instance, come to the conclusion of many others that the writings of Charles Dickens held the key to alleviating—perhaps even ending—England's social problems. But the owner of a tree nursery, who became interested in him, and gave him books he had not been able to afford, forced him to lower his enthusiasm for Dickens a few notches. "His characters," said the nursery owner, "are always either extremely wealthy and gentle, or poor and timid, or vicious. And his premise is that poverty in England will vanish if England's wealthy people become so impressed by his books they will start acting like his characters.

He hasn't written a word about the economic realities which have created poverty."

My friend William spent many hours with the tree nursery owner, Andrew Gosman, during the years he was with the newspaper. Gosman was (excuse the cliche) a walking encyclopedia. He told William his interest in him came from reading his byline stories in the paper and learning from the publisher that the reporter was self-educated.

When William left the paper seven years later he was, he told me, fired up with enthusiasm because the tree nursery owner had given him the key to acquiring knowledge. It was simply this: To understand a problem, one must understand why it became a problem. In other words, ask not why people get divorces, ask only why they get married. You will then find—if you eliminate the prevailing romantic nonsense—that it is the irresistible three-letter word S-E-X. Under a heavy cloud of sex, common sense vanishes, and people see qualities in each other that do not really exist. Ergo:

Divorce for the following reasons: "She threw waffles at me during breakfast," or "He insisted on the dog sleeping with us." (Note: These explanations were actual allegations in divorce complaints during William's years covering the courthouse. The complaint of one of his own former wives was that he admired and talked a lot about Schopenhauer—the gloomy German philosopher.)

When I asked him if he could explain his own razzle-dazzle life with women and a half-dozen divorces, he pretended anger and almost shouted:

"You should wash your mouth out with soap. You want I should act traditional? I want you should know I tried it. With two of my wives I didn't even go to bed before we were married, but it also ended in divorce."

My daughter Flora Mae tried to console me. "Dad," she said, "it wasn't a total loss. Remember you won all the arguments."

Then he became serious. He said he changed when he met Andrew Gosman and began to realize that

Journalism was just another job and not a mission to alter the world.

"Ad astra, per aspera (to the stars through privation)," said Gosman.

"The trouble with the stars is that when you think you're a mile nearer to them, you find they've drawn a mile away." They often talked about the difficulties one can expect living in a world dedicated to traditional lifestyles.

Only in your private life, in your own home, Gosman told him, can you consider yourself absolutely free. You can piss on the floor or do any other outrageous thing you wish. But don't forget: When you invite someone into your home or get married, that freedom is cut in half. You will find that you will have to lie or pick your words carefully, as will perhaps your guest or wife. So, unless everyone's interests are limited to watching "Hollywood Squares" or "Let's Make A Deal," you will have to pick your words and lie if you want to live peacefully. A home, said Gosman, should mirror the personalities of those who live in it—it is absolutely the only place where you can unburden yourself. A home, said the Canadian poet Robert Service, "is not four walls and a roof above, it also needs a woman's love."

In 1985, William appealed to me for help. He revealed that in the 1970's he became aware that the cells of an artery feeding oxygen to the sensory part of the brain were dying and the medical prognosis was that the dying cells would increase at a progressive rate. Now they reached a point where he was having trouble bringing words to the surface to express his thoughts. He was involved, he told me, in a lawsuit over a manuscript that involved Warren Beatty and Paramount Pictures and needed me to take care of some legal matters. My entire family joined in helping him, and I have been, what he calls, his "right hand" ever since.

Now in his 92nd year, he continues punching away on his 50-year-old Underwood. When I turn up and we talk, he sometimes shifts gears in the middle of a sentence with: "You want to hear a funny story? There was this handsome caretaker of an apartment house celebrating his 37th birthday with a bottle of scotch. At 5 p.m. he button-holed a tenant on his way to his apartment from work, and insisted the tenant have a few drinks with him.

While drinking he began to boast about his prowess with women. 'I have been in bed with every woman in this apartment house, except one. How do you like that?' he boasted. That evening during dinner, the tenant repeated the boast to his wife. And his wife said: "You say he said 'except one'? That must be that stuck-up Mrs. Wilson on the third floor."

Sometimes I chide him. "You know, William," I've told him, "You say that there can't possibly be a beginning to all the worlds and the constellations because Herman Von Helmholtz, the German physicist, says nothing is ever destroyed. Everything changes into something else—gas, water, steam, etcetera. So how can you create things that can't be destroyed? I don't get it. I think you're crazy."

"So I'm crazy and you're sane," he's replied. "So tell me, Mister Sane. Why is one of America's favorite four-letter words, f-u-c-k which is related to creating new life, forbidden while the four-letter word k-i-l-l which is related to destroying life, not forbidden? I'll tell you. If the word 'kill' was forbidden, no one would watch television."

That's my friend William.

REACHING FOR THE STARS

Warren Beatty and Kaiser, Too

IF THERE IS ANY COMMON denominator in the newspaper fraternity, it is that everyone, with hardly any exception, yearns and hopes that he or she will someday be able to write a book. And I was no exception. As a matter of fact, I was a member in the media—many of us in those days often referred to journalism as a newspaper racket—for only about three years when I began planning in my mind just such a project.

It was going to be called GOD'S MISTAKES, with God Himself as the protagonist. It was going to begin with God telling His Only Son that He had become bored with the sameness of all the millions of planets and constellations whirling eternally in space and so had decided to do some experimenting. He picked a scruffy, tiny planet, one that would never be missed, and added a little coloring to it with trees and other growing shrubs. Then He created animals and things like that so that their moving around would mean the planet was still there. The rest is biblical history.

GOD'S MISTAKES, He admitted, was in approving Noah's proposal to save two of everything He had created before the big flood. "My second mistake," said God sadly, "was in sending You, My only begotten Son, to try and redeem a bunch of savages." In the last chapter, I had in mind having an uncircumcised atheist fighting it out with Satan for control of what was left of God's Creation. I got the whole idea from a book that had become popular about the time I broke into journalism. It was called Heavenly Discourse and was written by Charles Erskine Scott Wood.

But in the last half of the 1940's when Anna Roosevelt, whom I served as a ghostwriter, urged me to write a book about myself and my family, I began to hedge. She had become aware that the scripts I had written for her contained material which appeared to come from sources not usually available through normal research. When she learned that some of it came from my family's involvement, her insistence that I write a book increased. She said it would be helpful to future researchers.

"Anna," I kept saying, "I am still searching for I don't know what." I haven't achieved anything. I am living with my third, or is it fourth wife, and haven't any sort of a feeling of security. I wanted to become an interpreter during the war, because they desperately needed Russian interpreters, but I was rejected because interpreting is in the intelligence field and I didn't have a college degree to qualify as an officer. All I ever wanted was a home with a wife and a couple of children. Forget the book, Anna, please. I can't tell you how much I appreciate your interest."

At three a.m. the following morning my telephone rang. It was Anna.

"I have a terrific idea," she shouted excitedly, "write a book called Reaching for the Stars. You know, nobody ever reaches the stars, but many of us try. The stars you see keep moving away inch by inch as you move inch by inch toward them. Wasn't it Oscar Wilde who said all of us live in the gutter, but some of us keep our eyes on the stars?"

During the years that followed her radio program's end because of her rheumatic fever attack, I continued getting letters from her in which she often suggested titles for a book. Twenty years later, an opportunity presented itself to begin research on a book about a beautiful woman, who was involved in many historically significant events that Anna wanted me to write about. It was an opportunity I could not resist. It was a biography of Louise Bryant, in whose life Warren Beatty was interested for a movie.

***

I think of everything that has happened to me, some of it rather weird, that the time I spent in 1973 talking with Warren Beatty in his penthouse in the Beverly-Wilshire Hotel has to be rated as the most interesting experience of my many years as a newsboy, farm laborer, railroader, musician and journalist. Up until then, I had always given top billing to the day I managed to penetrate Henry Kaiser's "palace guard" and be hired to write an unusual coast to coast radio news commentary.

Henry Kaiser was, after all, only a nice old man with a lot of money.

(I discovered that he really didn't know to what lengths some of his people went to keep others away from him when they decided, on their own, that those wishing to see him had no important business with their boss.) But Warren Beatty was something else. He was at that time one of the most sought after actors in the motion picture industry, and also the most difficult to get to see and hold still for an interview. As a matter of fact, the women members of the Los

Angeles news media once awarded him the "Sour Apple" for being near the head of the list of uncooperative stars in the motion picture industry. And little wonder that he is so much sought after. Immediately after his 1960 smash hit "Splendor in the Grass," he was able to brush aside $200,000 picture offers. He has been involved with some of the most beautiful women in the world. And nobody, except perhaps his business manager, knew exactly how much money his box office success, "Bonnie and Clyde," brought him. I specifically asked him that question and he said he didn't know.

Dear Anna:

"Ad astra, per aspera"—to the stars, through adversity, I will never make it to the heavenly stars. But I have managed to reach one star—a most important star in the entire motion picture industry's constellation.
So it all hasn't been a total loss, has it, Anna?

When I contemplate my past, as I do quite often these days, I see that the only time when I was what I would call successful was when I had the good fortune to come in contact with individuals who did not cling to traditional ways of achieving goals.

For instance, Eleanor Roosevelt refused to accept the meat industry as a sponsor for our program because that might inhibit her if it became necessary to attack the industry. So we remained unsponsored. Warren Beatty decided to name a thirty-three million dollar motion picture "Reds" at a time when the very sound of the word set mainstream America's blood boiling. And Henry Kaiser? Well, I once asked him to tell me what his favorite joke was. I said I might use it on one of our programs. He said it was about an efficiency expert who died, and as six pallbearers were carrying the coffin from the church to the hearse, he suddenly sat us and said, "If you put wheels on this thing, you can lay off a couple of these guys." If that isn't innovation, I don't know what is.

I was myself joking when I said he "was just an old man with a lot of money." Henry Kaiser was a man with a great love for people, and I think a lot of heads would have rolled if he had known that his well-meaning assistants were keeping people and their complaints away from him. It was John Gunther, the author of such books as Inside Europe, Inside Asia, and Inside U.S.A. who described Kaiser and his wife perfectly when he wrote that they make you think of a comfortable pair of house slippers.

And indeed they do. If you saw them walking together you would think that this remarkable multi-millionaire industrialist and his wife were a couple of senior citizens on their way to a senior citizens center to play pinochle or listen to a thirty-six year old bosomy lady lecture on "How to Grow Old Gracefully." Mrs. Kaiser didn't like airplanes and wouldn't let Henry fly on one. One day when I was in New York, Henry Kaiser, Jr., invited me to have lunch with him and his mother at the swanky, luxurious Plaza Hotel. It was a fantastic place, with prices to match. I joked about the prices on the menu and asked if toothpicks were extra. I then asked him if he and his mother ate at the Plaza Hotel often. "Oh, no," said Henry Junior, "we eat here only because Harry's Hot Dog Eatery is being picketed and mother will not cross the picket line."

***

How did I become involved with Henry Kaiser? It was this way. I had a hard time for more than a year after I was fired from the Folger's Coffee sponsored radio show for calling Franco of Spain a "schlemiel." I tried unsuccessfully to interest agencies in programs—one titled "Petticoat Press," with a woman reading the news, another a news program devoted entirely to Los Angeles news, a third to financial news, a fourth in which students would question important national leaders. All were crazy ideas in the 1940's. One day I learned that Henry Kaiser, Jr., had invited newspaper people to Fontana, east of Los Angeles, to inspect the new Kaiser plant that had been built on land that had been orange orchards for years. I joined the party and returned home with pamphlets and other mementos of the trip, including the address of Henry Junior's office in downtown Los Angeles. I bought a copy of the L.A. Times and began work on a fifteen minute news broadcast based on that day's news. It was the same kind of a news program I had written for Folger's Coffee, but I "pitched" it for Henry Kaiser's consumption.

You see, I knew a great deal about Henry Kaiser. I knew about his early years in Spokane, which go back to the days he owned a small photo shop and a gravel business, his role in building Grand Coulee Dam and other dams, and the many news stories about him that I handled while I was with newspapers. But most important, I knew all about his top priority: To restructure the present production-distribution process by which the manufacturing plants were in the east and the natural resources in the west.

This made it necessary for the west to pay the cost of shipping the resources east and pay again to have the finished products returned. I wrote a couple of special items, one datelined San Francisco and the other Portland, Oregon, in which Henry Kaiser's views were reflected.

It was a long shot, but what did I have to lose? I decided that the only chance I had of getting Henry Kaiser to become interested in the script was by making a recording, for he surely must get hundreds of written ideas for various projects. To make a recording I needed a top-rated announcer, because I was the fall-guy in the Schlemiel-Franco ruckus, and Frank Hemingway continued reading what someone else wrote. This time the announcer would have to avoid saying anything that might offend someone's wife, neighbor, boss, and most important, the sponsor and his wife, neighbor, etc., etc. I was fortunate in talking a handsome Mormon bishop names Wendell Noble into making the recording. He was everything Frank Hemingway was, and more.

In those days, the fall of 1947, there was still only one size record available, and it required three of them for a full news script. My hope was that I might be able to interest Henry Junior in the records, and that I might induce him to have his father hear them.

***

Henry Junior's office was on the southwest corner of Pershing Square in the heart of downtown Los Angeles. It wasn't much of an office. Junior was alone, behind an office desk with a newspaper in his hand. There was a typewriter stand and a typewriter, but no sign of a typist. I introduced myself and said I had some records and I thought he might be interested in hearing them. I went on to explain, in as few sentences as possible, what they were all about. He said he would take them home and play them, but when I mentioned his father, he said, "Not a chance. Every agent of commentators and newscasters, including Walter Winchell, has tried to interest father in radio, but he will not even consider sponsoring them."

I was disappointed and depressed, but I stayed on, hoping that if he himself heard the records, he might find them interesting enough to ask his father to hear them. He was an interesting individual anyway, this son of a multi-millionaire, and seemed eager to talk about himself. The most important thing I learned was that he was afflicted with multiple sclerosis, which seemed to explain the tiny office. It was just a place from which to arrange some occasional projects as the invitation of newspapermen to visit the Kaiser steel plan in Fontana.

It was a good investment of my time. Before I left he said, "I am flying to New York this weekend and I'll take the records with me." Five days later my telephone rang and I heard the voice of Henry Junior. "Dad liked it and wants to see you here next Wednesday with Wendell Noble and your manager (manager? what manager?). The transportation office will call you when it has arranged for transportation and the hotel. Good luck." I had no trouble finding somebody to be a manager.

***

The conference to work out all the practical details for getting the program on six hundred and forty radio stations was something to remember.

I found myself in a longer conference room than I had ever seen on the hundredth floor of a New York skyscraper, home of the Mutual Broadcasting System. I felt sure something big and important was about to happen. But like a virgin bride on her wedding night, I didn't know exactly what. At the long conference table were Joe Frazer, Henry Kaiser's partner in the Kaiser-Frazer (automobile) Corporation. Next to him was the network's news director, then Henry Kaiser himself, and beside him the representative of the Chicago advertising agency, which would be working with the network.

Along the wall, across from the conference table, was a string of about sixteen attorneys and other representatives of Kaiser Corporations.

I, Wendell, and the manager sat on chairs about ten feet from the conference table like three wet sheep huddled together for warmth. I sat staring at everyone with a weird feeling that I was dreaming. I was there, but felt as though it was someone else whom I could not easily identify.

The network's news director made clear almost at once his belief that Mr. Kaiser had made a mistake in sponsoring such a program. "You can get Mr. Winchell, Mr. Kaiser," he said. "He is available."

Mr. Kaiser responded, spacing his words: "I don't want Mr. Winchell.

I want these boys."

The director took another approach. "You know,

Mr. Kaiser, this may be a fluke. We often have people who come up with a good script. But when they have to write scripts one after another for days they flop."

This brought from the agency representative sitting next to Mr. Kaiser something that shook me up. "We can settle that by asking Mr. Greene to go down to the teletype room and write something which will show whether the script is a fluke. Do you mind, Mr. Greene?"

Did I mind! My God, I hadn't been in a teletype room for more than a year. The script was written at my leisure from the *L.A. Times*. Did I mind? I saw the whole project going down the drain. It was like the cartoons you see in The New Yorker. A fat, cigar smoking agent sitting behind his desk, says to a starving comedian standing before him, "So you're a comedian, so go ahead, make me laugh." I was shaking slightly as I made my way behind someone who was guiding me to the teletype room on the floor below.

Inside the room I saw the dozen or more teletype machines clicking and the yellow paper rolling into containers on the floor behind them. As I walked from one to another with a legal-size pad and pencil in my hand, it occurred to me that what I needed was an item that would appeal to both Mr. Kaiser and Joe Frazer. To hell with everyone else. When I glanced at the sports machine I caught the name Carl Furillo. I knew nothing about sports then and I know nothing about sports now. But the first letters in Carl Furillo, on the air, sound K.F.—Kaiser-Frazer. That was what I needed. I cut off the item. It was about the New York Yankees and the Brooklyn Dodgers, who were playing at Ebbets Field, and about Carl Furillo who had done something which upset the Dodgers and had created a tremendous uproar among Dodger fans.

I began writing a radio news item: "In the world of sports today, Carl Furillo failed his Brooklyn fans by stumbling at second and making the World Series a tie. The uproar—Kill Furillo, Kill Furillo, K.F., Kill Furillo, K.F.—even reached the United Nations where the Russians, believing the proletarian revolution had finally reached America, sent a messenger to Ebbets Field to determine who is K.F. (Pause) "Friends, this is Wendell Noble, I am not going to tell you who K.F. is, I will tell you WHAT it is. It is a Kaiser-Frazer automobile that will never fail you. Why not stop in at your nearby dealer and let him give you a ride in a K.F."

It was a ridiculous bit of nonsense, used unforgivingly, but it worked...it worked magnificently.

Wendell Noble, bless his Mormon heart, read it beautifully, and the advertising agency representative rose from his seat next to Henry Kaiser.

In a dramatic voice he said, "Mr. Greene, you have faced a challenge and met it beautifully." Then Mr. Kaiser addressed Joe Frazer: "Joe, you take one day for (slight pause) the K.F. car, (laughter) and I'll take three more for the steel plant."

I was still in and out of my dream world. They began talking about money for each day's program, and when they came to four programs for seven hundred dollars a week for each of us, Mr. Kaiser stopped the proceedings, looked in my direction and asked, "Bill, what do you think of the prices?"

I swallowed hard and said, "Mr. Kaiser, I don't know anything about money. I never heard of so much money for writing the news. Whatever you think is right is fine with me." Mr. Kaiser pointed a finger at one of the silent lawyers along the wall and said, "I want you to make sure this fellow is protected."

Before we left for home he said, "I want you boys to stop in Michigan and go over our automobile plant." And I said, "Certainly Mr. Kaiser, but I have to be in Burbank on Thursday. You see, Thursday is when I get my unemployment check."

Mr. Kaiser laughed. But I wasn't joking. The soles of my shoes had holes and I badly needed a new car battery.

***

The program went off the air after six months when the Kaiser people got into trouble with the Securities and Exchange Commission because someone "leaked" the news of a bond issue about to be floated by the giant Kaiser network. I never learned the details, but it became necessary to slash the advertising budget and our million dollar a year outlay for radio bit the dust.

I learned a good deal about the Kaiser family from Henry Junior, and his great love for his parents. I once asked Mr. Kaiser how many corporations he had, and he turned to his son and asked, "How many corporations have we got, Junior?" And Junior replied, "I think we have twenty-three, Dad." Several years later I happened to be in the San Francisco Bay area and dropped in at the Kaiser offices in Oakland to say hello. Henry Junior was in a wheelchair by this time, and the first thing he said to me was, "We got two more corporations, one in Hawaii and one here." I often accompanied him on visits to Kaiser employees who were sick, and to distribute Christmas gifts to the employees' home. At his own home in the huge Kaiser housing section near today's Los Angeles International Airport, I always found him exercising in the hope of controlling his dreadful affliction. His greatest worry throughout the year, he told me, was in figuring out how to surprise his parents on their yearly wedding anniversary. "Money becomes absolutely useless sometimes," moaned poor Henry Kaiser, Jr.

For our Christmas Day program, Mrs. Kaiser asked me to write something appropriately special. I wrote a three-minute story about two French soldiers wounded in the Franco-Prussian War, one of whom died Christmas Eve far away from home. She was delighted and we received hundreds of requests for copies. When Mrs. Kaiser was dying, I believe of cancer, she made her husband promise he would marry her nurse. And of that, to paraphrase the New Testament, you can surely say: "Greater love hath no woman."

HOW I MET WARREN BEATTY

Stop me if you've heard this one: At a British University an instructor in English told his students that the best way to assure reader interest in a short story is by writing about religion, royalty, or sex. One student took no chances and began his tale with: "For God's sake, your Majesty," cried the young woman, "remove your hand from my thigh!"

For me, the magic words were "Warren Beatty" when he became interested in my biography of Louise Bryant, the remarkable Portland woman portrayed by Diane Keaton in Beatty's movie, *REDS*. My involvement with Beatty tops all the events in my life. I had been trying unsuccessfully to create interest among publishers and motion picture people in the manuscript of my Bryant biography and, believe it or not, I got through to the motion picture industry's most inaccessible personality with no more than an eight-cent stamp.

Here is the scenario: It is a drizzly, depressing day in Tacoma, Washington. At four in the afternoon the telephone rings.

"Is this William M. Greene?"

"Ye–e–ss."

"This is Warren Beatty in Beverly Hills. I just got through reading the stuff you sent. Pretty interesting material."

I was surprised at how excited I felt and said, "I'm certainly glad, Mr. Beatty."

"What in hell are you doing in a place like Tacoma writing about John Reed, Eugene O'Neill, and Louise Bryant and Russian revolutionaries?" he asked.

I gave him a quick summary of my background: some thirty years in the Los Angeles–Hollywood area in radio, television, and newspapers, how I moved to Tacoma after the Hearsts began their union-busting campaign at the Los Angeles Herald-Examiner where I had been working. I told him that I had ghostwritten a radio program for Eleanor and Anna Roosevelt and had done some speech writing for Jimmy Roosevelt when he ran for governor of California against Earl Warren. He, in turn, told me that he had plans for a picture about the life of John Reed. "Oh," I said, "you're going to take that De Laurentis offer." (The Italian producer had been trying to interest Beatty in such a project.)

He said he wouldn't even think of it. It would be a Russian propaganda film, he thought, and he wanted no part of it. "I've been interested in John Reed for a long time," he said. "In fact, I have a screenplay written, but this stuff you sent me . . . I may make some changes."

I told him that I had been planning a trip to Los Angeles (so I fudged a little) and asked if I might meet and talk with him. He said no, explaining that I would have to sign a paper before he could do that, in order to avoid legal complications. It's to protect the distributors," he said, adding that when Bonnie and Clyde was released they faced more than two hundred lawsuits from people claiming they had come up first with the original idea for the film. "But I'll tell you what," he said. "I'll get hold of my lawyer and have him prepare the paper. When you arrive, call the Beverly Wilshire Hotel, and if I'm not in ask for my secretary. She'll set up a date."

I thought it was the usual brush-off, but he called

back four hours later. Only then did I begin to realize what had happened. It was a delayed reaction, like when you're driving along and a child dashes out from behind a parked car; you swerve, missing the child by an inch. A dozen blocks away you stop suddenly and your hands are shaking because you've just realized how close you came to killing that child.

Hearing from Warren Beatty was almost as incredible as the call I got from New York back in 1947, the call telling me that the millionaire industrialist, Henry Kaiser, wanted to talk to me. Crazy, man! Crazy! I think God was sorry and doing penance for the way He ignored me during my childhood years in czarist Russia.

Before I go on to describe my three sessions with Mr. Beatty in his Beverly Hills penthouse, I must tell you something about my Louise Bryant manuscript, whose motion picture rights Beatty acquired from me. I spent nearly five years researching material to reconstruct the life of this remarkable woman from the day she was born in San Francisco in 1885 to her death in Paris in 1936. Very little was known of her, for early in life she developed the habit of always creating new images of herself. She died destitute, alone and forgotten, her last tragic years spent as a lesbian, prostitute, drug addict and hopeless alcoholic. But even ten years before her death, she was still a remarkably beautiful woman who was involved, in one way or another, in an amazing number of historically significant events, many of which are pertinent to our time.

Among the numerous men with whom she was involved, three were particularly important, and one was especially important to Warren Beatty. They were:

Eugene O'Neill the great American playwright, whose affair with her made an abortion necessary and also became the basis for his prize-winning play, "Strange Interlude", Her third husband William C. Bullitt, the Philadelphia millionaire, who was named America's first ambassador to the Soviet Union by his friend Franklin Roosevelt, and John Reed, son of a wealthy Oregon pioneer family who became a revolutionary and lies buried in the Kremlin Wall in Moscow as a Soviet hero. It was Louise's five stormy years with John Reed that Beatty needed for his projected motion picture about the Russian Revolution, for both were eyewitnesses to the upheaval that jolted civilization in a new direction.

She was a correspondent for the Hearst papers; she knew and wrote about Lenin, Trotsky, Kerensky, Mussolini and a score of other world leaders; she knew Sigmund Freud, both personally and as a patient; she defied Congressional Committees investigating radicalism; she went on hunger strikes while in jail during the struggle for womens' political rights, and she shook up the University of Oregon campus, while a student there, by appearing in public wearing transparent blouses, and as the first woman to wear lipstick in public.

One of the most unusual features was my discovery that while she headed deeper and deeper into revolution and violence, a brother became one of the nation's top business executives and an important member of the Eisenhower administration.

Dear Mr. B.G. : If you have a millionaire American ambassador with an alcoholic, lesbian wife, why do you need Warren Beatty? Everybody knows that people

would rather see her in a peekaboo blouse than running around in a revolution.
Just N. Curious

Dear Just Curious: That's a good question. It reminds me of a story about a Jewish composer who fled Hitler's Germany and was hired by a Hollywood studio to provide background music for movies. One day he was asked to do that for a scene in which a huge wheat field is in the grip of a raging storm. The roaring 130 mile wind has crushed the waist-high grain to the ground, and an endless stream of lightning bolts, punctuated by earth-shaking thunder, splits the heavy dark clouds. We see no buildings or animals, only a pregnant peasant woman. Her body bent against the wind, she is struggling, inch by inch, to reach a resting place. Suddenly she collapses and the camera reveals the triumphant fact that with willpower and determination man can handle everything ruthless nature can dish out. The peasant woman has brought a new life into the world. "Mazltov! Mazltov!" "With all that going on," says our timid little Jewish composer, "Why do you need music?"
Cordially yours,
B.G.

I needed Warren Beatty, even though his interest in the Louise Bryant biography manuscript centered on only one phase of her sensation-filled life.

You see, there are usually two prerequisites for a biography—either the author or the person about whom he or she is writing, or both, must be well known. In this case, Louise Bryant was a familiar name only to those who read books about John Reed or Eugene O'Neill and one or two others who had known or been involved with her. My own credentials were even skimpier.

So the manuscript was rejected by publisher after publisher. It became clear to me that only an F. Scott Fitzgerald-style writer could overcome the obstacles I faced, for if anyone's real life ever paralleled the lives of Fitzgerald's fictional characters, it was Louise Bryant's.

I had not considered the movies a possible way to generate publisher interest in the Louise Bryant biography, before Evelyn Scott came along and said: "Let me handle this."

Evelyn is an actress—she was Ada Jacks, the tavern owner in the television series Peyton Place—and a longtime friend.

Now she picked up her copy of the Louise Bryant manuscript and took it to the office of Albert Ruddy, the producer of the highly successful picture, THE GODFATHER, and "ordered" him to read it. (There was a time, she told me, when both of them stood in line to collect their social security unemployment checks.)

A couple of weeks passed and I received a letter from Ruddy, which among other things said, "I totally enjoyed reading it." I knew he was telling the truth, for if he hadn't Evelyn would have sent him a questionnaire to fill out: What was Louise's father's first name? What did Trotsky say to her about his wife? When did she begin drinking? Did she have an affair with John Reed's artist friend Andrew Dasburg?

But he wasn't very encouraging. He said only a top-name woman star or director who became personally interested in Louise Bryant's life could get the project off the ground as a motion picture.

While pondering this pronouncement, I received a news clipping from a New York friend which said

the Italian producer Dino De Laurentis was planning a motion picture based on John Reed's *Ten Days
That Shook The World* and was trying to get Warren
Beatty to accept the role of Reed. I knew that if Beatty
agreed, he would surely be interested in material
about the most important woman in Reed's life—
material that was unavailable anywhere else. But I
also knew that my chances of letting Warren Beatty
know I had such material, were about the same as
wining the Irish Sweepstakes during the days before
lottery mania gripped America.

But what did I have to lose? A stamp cost only
eight cents in 1973. I had an extra copy of a five-
page outline of the manuscript's contents, and a Screen
Actors Guild directory provided the name of Beatty's
agency.

On Friday, January 28, 1973, I added a brief "Dear
Mr. Beatty" note and mailed the letter to:

Warren Beatty
c/o the William Morris Agency, Inc.
151 El Camino
Los Angeles, California 90212

Ten days later on February 7, 1973 he called me.

It was a miracle, for the task of agencies with clients of top stars is not to hustle jobs for their clients,
but to keep would-be authors and geniuses with brilliant
ideas away from them.

If your idea of a movie star's life away from the
studio cameras is based on the pictures and glamor-
ous descriptions in Sunday newspaper supplements
and movie fan magazines— lovely Spanish-style homes,
beautiful young women scattered about a large swimming
pool—you can forget it, insofar as Warren Beatty,

and his penthouse atop the Beverly Wilshire Hotel is concerned.

The hotel is on Wilshire Boulevard in the heart of the business district in Beverly Hills. It is a ten- story building, if you count the roof as one of the floors. Beatty's penthouse was on the roof , and I would say that it barely qualified under Webster's generous definition as "a small building in the roof of a larger edifice; sometimes used as a dwelling." The hotel's elevator went only to the eighth floor. You walked up to the ninth, a ghostly corridor reminiscent of a scene form Wuthering Heights, and then another flight of steep steps to a door with a sigh, *La Escondida*. You rang the doorbell, the door opened and there was Warren Beatty.

What I saw was a remarkably handsome, smiling man in rumpled slacks, a white shirt held together by the middle button, sandals on his feet, and his hair tied at the back with a narrow piece of ribbon. The second time I turned up, he had been sunbathing and had one of those big towels they advertise in the expensive slick-paper magazines around his stomach. I could see why he was often described as one of the most handsome and virile men in Hollywood.

The penthouse—the very word brought up erotic visions of clandestine avours in luxurious surroundings— was one big room covering half of the entire roof. It was divided by a large screen, on one side of which were doors to a kitchen and a bathroom. In the main part there was a Hollywood style sofa with a couple of bolsters, and in front of this a large coffee table, the top of which was loaded with books, manuscripts, unopened mail, bits of paper with penciled notations, a section of the *New York Times*, a telephone, a

tray with dishes containing leftover food, used nap-
kins and empty martini glasses which room service
had not yet removed.

The outstanding feature was the other half of the
roof; the terrace, with deck chairs, iron-legged tables,
several huge sun umbrellas, tall tropical plants in
large containers —a great place for sunbathing. From
here, on a clear day, one got a magnificent view of
Beverly Hills and the southwest part of Los Angeles.

***

There was a troubling dream-like quality about
the hours during the three afternoons I spent talking with him. Somewhere in the back of my mind
were a lot of unanswered questions which always
seemed to surface when I found myself on a personal
basis with very important people. What in hell was
I doing there? Why, when I came to Canada from
Russia as a child with my family, did I have to become
such a "chochom"—a wise guy. Why didn't I go to
school like everybody else did? If I wanted to get married,
why didn't I go into some kind of a business and find
a nice Jewish girl and raise a family like all the others
did? Why did I have to have so many wives?

So I sat as I always did, unable to get rid of the
vague, insecure feeling that I didn't belong there.
Oddly, I never had that feeling while interviewing
anyone for newspapers or magazine articles or similar
purposes. It was always in cases where I was personally involved. And here I was, Shmeryle Greenstein,
sitting there and talking to a millionaire who could
dial a number and have the most prestigious writers come running to him. Dear God!, don't let me

commit a faux pas. I did just that. "I didn't know you are Shirley MacLaine's brother." He was silent, and I became more uneasy. (I did not know at that time that he and his sister were not on the best of terms.) "I know it'll surprise you, but I never saw *Bonnie and Clyde.*" He smiled and I felt a little better.

There was nothing at all about him to justify my uneasiness. He has a most engaging, boyish grin and pleasant manner, and appears to be one of those remarkable people who, when they become interested in something, are thoroughly and completely absorbed in it, at least as long as the interest lasts. You need to be with him only an hour to get the feeling he has known you for years. This, I imagine, comes from his possession of what is known as "total recall." Casually mention an unimportant name, and two days later he will not have to say, "what did you say his name was?" He remembers. It will be you who has forgotten. Each time he prepared to call room service to bring up food he looked at me—I thought— anxiously and said, "Are you sure all you want is a corned beef on rye and a bottle of beer? I can't function unless I eat three times a day."

He seemed to become as interested in me as in the life of Louise Bryant and the unusual way I went about digging out details of her life. He wanted to know about my childhood in pogrom-ridden czarist Russia and everything else I was able to tell about myself. He was delighted when I told him I could still speak Russian and said, "Ya nyemnozh'ko govoroo po roose'kee." (passable translation—I speak a little Russian). I don't know if he learned his Russian because of his interest in John Reed and the Russian revolution, or from Maya Plisetskaya, the beautiful

Russian ballerina who sunbathed when in California, on his penthouse terrace.

I almost became embarrassed by his interest in me.
Helen Feibelmann, his secretary in an office on the
floor below, came into the room and Beatty said:
"Guess how many times this guy was married? No
less than six times." And when she called him by
phone he always said: "Tell him I'll call him."

When I told him about my former wife, Helen Smith,
who had helped me with the research for the manuscript, he said, "Bring her over tomorrow and we'll
all go out for lunch. But poor Helen, a linotype op-
erator, panicked. It would be like having lunch with
God. She found an excuse for not accepting the invitation. (I added the name of my former wife Helen
Smith (now deceased) to the contract, because we
had resumed a relationship and because of her valuable
research contribution.)

The contract itself was one of these seven-page,
single-spaced legal monstrosities, with the subject
and predicate divided by a half-dozen looping phrases.
Before signing it, Warren called his lawyer and said,
"What shall I do now?" When he put down the re-
ceiver, he found a pocket checkbook and made out
a check for $250, which he handed to me saying,
"You know, I would feel like a shit if this was all
the money you got, if we made a picture with Louise
Bryant in it."

I was on a heavenly cloud. I cannot tell you how
thrilled I was to see my name next to Warren Beatty's—
a seventy-five year old man, with little hope of ever
seeing in print the only worthwhile writing in his
long career—beside that of a world-renowned motion picture star. Warren would surely not forget

my life in Russia and find a role for me somewhere in the screenplay about the revolution, and he had promised to help get the manuscript published. "We will find an agent with clout and get it off the ground," he told me.

All my problems were over. The contract? Warren, you will remember, said he needed it to protect the distributors of movies from a flood of "nuisance lawsuits" against producers that usually follow the release of motion pictures. The very idea that someone who was as interested in me, admired me, and liked me as Warren Beatty did, would do something contrary to my welfare was ridiculous. And there was the $250 check, which to me was clearly "a token   payment," like "earnest money" when you buy a new home. Boy oh boy! Was I naive!

On the afternoon of the third day I was ready to leave for home. He accompanied me to the head of the stairs outside the door of *La Escondida*, and as I started bouncing down the stairs, the contract and check in my briefcase, he shouted, "Hey there, take it easy. I'll want you to do some more research, and *don't* want you to have a heart attack." As I looked back at him rather surprised, the thought seemed to occur to him that I may have interpreted what he said as a reflection on my age. He grinned and added "You know, I wouldn't dare go bouncing down those stairs that way myself."

It did not take long for news of my good fortune to spread in my neighborhood. Some of my neighbors and fellow workers on the *Tacoma News Tribune* knew that I was working on a book because of the many days I was away from my home and my job doing research. But the news that Warren Beatty had acquired the motion picture rights to my book, came as a stunning surprise. They began turning up at my place to congratulate me. My Jewish friends said "mazltov," and everyone slapped me on the back and told me what a lucky old bastard I was.

It was not long before I discovered, to my chagrin, that nearly all of them, especially the women and their teenage daughters, were interested far more in Warren Beatty than in me. They made bantering inquiries about how I was going to spend all the money they were certain I had collected; a few asked what sort of a motion picture Beatty had in mind, and, as a kind of after-thought, all wanted to know how someone like me managed to get an inaccessible star like Warren Beatty interested in the manuscript.

Beatty was at that time still a mystery. Most of what was known about his private life came from the gossip columns and scandal peddlers. Movie fans were fed an amazing and lurid amount of information about him, none of which contained the smallest grain of truth—he was a communist, a sadist, had illegitimate children at home and abroad, had seduced scores of women, and, among other things, headed the list of men the Los Angeles vice squad had constantly under close surveillance.

Little wonder, then , that I suddenly found myself in the limelight—at least among friends, neighbors, fellow newspaper workers and casual acquaintances. Not so much because I was now the author of a book to which an important actor-producer had obtained the motion picture rights, but because they had learned that I had spent a good deal of time talking with him in his Beverly Hills hotel penthouse.

Here I was, a nondescript old man working in a small newspaper, back from the glamour capitol of the world with a contract and a Xerox copy of Warren Beatty's personal check. Normally someone like me would have been expected to come back from a Los Angeles vacation and boast that he had seen Archie Bunker walk into the CBS Studio on Fairfax Avenue.

So it is not surprising that they came to my place to drink beer and eat smoked fish, some to chat and some to learn "the truth," so they thought, about the man who skyrocketed to fame immediately after appearing in *Splender in the Grass* and became one of the film industry's top moneymakers. They were sure I would be able to satisfy their craving for Hollywood glamour and vicarious thrills.

Was it true that he turns down quarter-million dollar offers to do movies? Did he say anything about Leslie Caron? And did I think he was really ditched by Joan Collins to live with Leslie? What about Natalie Wood? Why did he never get married? Is it true that he and his sister Shirley MacLaine don't talk to each other? Did I get to meet any of his beautiful women?

They were so eager to know the most intimate details of his personal life, they would have believed the most preposterous things I could have dreamed up. It was, however not necessary for me to do that. Anything I could say about him was news and listened to, especially since it had never appeared in print—what his home looked like, how he was dressed, how he acted when not before studio cameras, how he ordered lunch from room service. It was all just as interesting as was my report that on one occasion as I arrived, a remarkably beautiful young woman with delicate features was pulling on her long gloves as she prepared to leave. "Was she . . . was she there all night do you suppose?" asked the wife of one of the fellows on the paper, her voice, I thought, trembling. I said, well, I am sure she wasn't there to give Warren piano lessons.

Time passed, and by January 30, 1976, the hard facts began to sink in.

I became fully aware that as soon as I was out of sight and Warren Beatty had reentered his penthouse, I became to him just one among the many people to whom he was inaccessible. I resigned myself to the hard fact that I was taken for a ride and that all I had was the publication rights to the manuscript and a photocopy of a $250 check, the original of which Helen used to pay the rent for her apartment.

But I kept getting news clippings from friends in Hollywood and New York indicating that Warren Beatty's plans for a movie about John Reed were still on the front burner, so I waited and hoped. I wasn't going to let him off the hook so easily.

It is all spelled out in Part IV of the January 30, 1976 edition of the *Los Angeles Times* by the paper's arts director Charles Champlin, who interviewed Warren Beatty in his penthouse. The article is titled BEATTY AND THE BEAST.

Nothing seems to have changed in the penthouse in the three years except for the addition of a third telephone. Champlin found Beatty the way I found him. "He reenters the room carrying a mug of tea, and fishes a crumpled envelope from the wastebasket for the tea bag," wrote Champlin. Remember, I said there were empty martini glasses on the coffee table when I turned up.

The article itself is "high road" stuff, written for artists during the nation's "let's make love, not war" era, and is replete with such phrases as "sexual publicity mills," "the contemporary compulsive," "built-in lack of dignity" and "heavy sub-plot."

But there is one that justifies the title *Beatty and the Beast*. It is one, I think you will agree, that justifies my own idea for a title: HOW I WAS SHAMPOOED BY WARREN BEATTY. Here are Champlin's words:

"There are no more than a dozen superstars, and Beatty is one of them. He is also like no other. Beneath the boyish grin is a relentless negotiator, a very skillful manipulator, a tireless and inspired promoter of films he believes in and has a stake in, and a steel-willed achiever."

I guess I'm lucky, he didn't deduct the cost of the beer and corned beef on rye. Praise the Lord!

A GUIDE TO BECOMING INFORMED

WARNING: Becoming informed may be dangerous to your peace of mind. You may start worrying about things that never bothered you before.

I AM SERIOUS ABOUT the consequences of becoming informed. Take, for instance, a cow standing in a field and chewing her cud. She doesn't worry about whether other cows have anything to chew. The cow will, of course, always be that way, because she was created without the ability to experience empathy for the plight of others. But not so with people. For example, you may have always considered yourself a charitable person. You gave the Salvation Army your old clothes, and put your spare coins into those little containers at checkout stands in stores, and never forgot the less fortunate at Thanksgiving and Christmas. You are, as a matter of fact, rather proud of your charitable record.

One day you happen to come across a phrase in a book which is attributed to Jack London: "Charity is not giving a dog a bone, it's sharing one with him." You look up the word in the dictionary and to your amazement learn that your definition of the word charity is the fourth in a long list of definitions, all of them related to the welfare of others. You now have a lot to worry about, including your income tax deductions for charitable contributions.

***

There is a wrong way to become informed and

there is a right way. Let us first take the wrong way: There was this sexy blonde who complained bitterly: "I got a brain and a mind like you," said she ungrammatically, "but all that men are interested in is my body. Why can't they like me for my mind also?"

"If you start reading books," she was told, "you will become informed and popular and you will be able to take part in important discussions, and everyone will admire you for being both beautiful and clever."

Well, one evening she found herself at a reception. Well-dressed men and women were standing in groups, each with a martini in his or her hand, discussing various matters. She was in one such group, and at one point saw an opportunity to become popular by submitting her opinion: "I think it is terrible the way they treated Marie Antoinette, don't you?"

Now for the right way of becoming informed, which might help in understanding why we have disputes, conflicts, hates, myths, and only God knows what else.

We will introduce the views of three important people in this discussion; Aristotle, the Greek philosopher who lived three centuries before the birth of Christ, Rene Descartes, the seventeenth century French philosopher, who is the "father" of the theory called rationalism, and our own President Abe Lincoln.

I don't know about you, but I divide into two groups the words we use to communicate with each other. One is CONCRETE and the other is ABSTRACT.

The concrete words are names for such things as a chair, book, automobile, flower, knife, machine, house, bridge, tomato, bread, and a million other things. All can be different, all can be used in many ways, but everybody knows what they are. A loaf of bread is "khlyeb" in Russian, "pan" in Spanish, "brot" in German, "brait" in Yiddish (Jonathan Swift in "Gulliver's Travels" called bread "the staff of life")— the important thing is that nobody will question what a loaf of bread is.

That is not the case with abstract words such as virtue, patriotism, loyalty, love, hate, heroism, evil, compassion, and most important of all, truth. They do not mean the same thing to everyone. Far, far from it. All of our disputes, conflicts and quarrels, between nations as well as individuals, can be traced to the differing interpretations of these words and hundreds like them. You see, among the many definitions of the word abstract itself is this: "Existing in the mind only." This means that an individual's background (what he has read, how he was brought up, his religious convictions, his dedication to free enterprise, his social stature), all these play a part in the way he interprets abstract words. Is there a better explanation for a president of the United States calling his budget compassionate while others say it's about as compassionate as Scrooge giving a shilling to a poorhouse? Why do some Americans call Nicaraguan rebels freedom fighters and others call them terrorists? Why do five Supreme Court Judges, who claim to be objective, say a law is constitutional, and four others, equally objective, perhaps even graduates from the same universities, say it is not constitutional? Why are some disgusted by a hunter spending enough money to feed a hundred hungry children for five years, traveling thousands of miles just to kill tigers, and others envying him as a heroic sportsman? Is the Soviet Union really an "evil empire"? Is the United States a land dominated by Wall Street and capitalist exploiters determined to crush the proletariat?

You know what Abe Lincoln said? "Calling a cow's tail a leg doesn't make a cow a five- legged animal."

***

Truth! What is truth? During the only time in my life when I had to appear in a courtroom, not as a reporter, but as a defendant in my own divorce case, my former wife flared up. "Are you calling me a liar?" she demanded of my attorney. "I didn't say that," said the attorney, the late Gerald Levie. "I said that you made up the truth as you went along."

Let us see what Aristotle had to say about this most crucially important word "truth." He said that there cannot be two sides to a statement, any more than one can be both awake and asleep at the same time.

The statement can't be both true and false. There can only be two individuals, each one claiming that his interpretation is the true one.

This doesn't help us much, because we have just been discussing why, so to speak, "one man's meat is another man's poison." Let us see what Rene Descartes has to say.

Descartes was a philosopher and a mathematician. He believed in acquiring knowledge by reasoning and not faith, which depends on the writing or words of another. What was unique about Rene's style of reasoning was its basis in mathematics. This made his conclusions doubt-proof throughout the world: 2 x 2 is 4. It can't be anything else, because you can take one tomato, then another, then another, then another, and you have four tomatoes. Similarly, a square board can't be anything but a square board because you can see it, or if you're blind, feel the four sides.

It was with these indisputable conclusions that he decided to his, if not to many others, satisfaction that there is a God. What is important here is not that Rene Descartes discovered God, for God is being discovered daily: "How I Learned to Swim and Found God," "How I met Warren Beatty and Found God"—what is important is that the method he used in reaching the conclusion about God became known as rationalism—a system for thinking and reaching conclusions.

Descartes wasn't searching for God. He was searching for a single abstract statement that could not be doubted by anyone. It would then be the "true" side of the question Aristotle talked about. It would be the TRUTH for which all philosophers have been searching. He spent days and nights, but always drew blanks. You could not even say, "when you drop a stone it will fall to the ground." The best you can say is "it always fell to the ground and will probably fall to the ground again," but there is no way you can be sure "it is true that it will again fall to the ground."

Finally, Descartes said, "I think that the only thing I cannot doubt is that I am Rene Descartes." Thus, he developed the principle "I think, therefore I exist," for if he doubted his existence, he would not have been around to do the doubting, would he? Then he reasoned that if his existence is in his mind, his mind's existence must be in a greater mind. You guessed it—God's. Two centuries later a Dane named Soren Kierkegaard found a flaw in the man's-mind-tied-to-God theory. It did not make man fully responsible for his behavior. He developed a theory called "existentialism," based on the principle, "I exist, therefore I think."

Whatever happened to rationalism, it seems to have been a good way to find who's right and who's wrong?" you ask, eager to find more things to worry about.

Well, a funny thing happened. You know how carefully Descartes worked to reach a conclusion, step-by-step, making sure that 2 x 2 always equals 4?

Well, now we don't do that. Instead, we create the conclusion first, then rationalize our way step-by-step toward justification. It began with Lenin.

At the height of the 1917 upheaval, posters and leaflets all over Russia read: Comrades, grab the land, grab the factories. We'll make it legal later." That's the only time Lenin was honest.

We give bonuses today to people who agree to ask for American help to overthrow regimes we don't like. The justification for doing that often parallels the sad case of a poor little rabbit about to be devoured by a wolf, who claimed that the rabbit's brother tried to attack him. "But I don't have a brother," sobbed the rabbit. "Well," snarled the wolf, "if you did have one he would have attacked me."

We have ended this epic analysis of man's search for truth. I am sorry rationalism lost its popularity. So many questions remain unanswered that the slightest contribution to understanding is a plus. Why do we know the way cells act, but not why they do it? Why do we get such a thrill when a fish struggles for its life on a hook, and the more it struggles to stay alive, the greater the thrill? Why can't we stop an orgasm once it starts?

Why must we be unconscious for a sizable portion of a twenty-four hour day instead of staying awake and just relaxing? Why do we attribute so much to our minds when the dictionaries tell us only what the mind does, and not what it is? In various ways they say: "It is that which powers the intellect" or "it is that which enables man to distinguish between right and wrong." And if all that doesn't give you enough to worry about, worry about why some live high off the hog and so many thank God if they can buy a jar of pickled pig knuckles.

CREDIT: HOW IT ALL BEGAN

Are These Legal Tender in Heaven?

SINCE "EASY CREDIT" PLAYED such an important port in the Great Depression, let us begin with those years. Recessions and depressions come with the free enterprise package. We used to distinguish between them by saying that in a recession you lose the belt that keeps your pants up, but in a depression you lose both your belt and your pants.

A great—if not the greatest—contribution to the disastrous severity of the Great Depression that began in the fall of 1929 can easily be traced to the government's "hands off" policy. It let "laissez faire" go berserk—it was an invitation to speculators to "come and get it," it was an automobile running downhill without brakes. Skyscrapers were built without the slightest assurance that there would be tenants to occupy them. Florida homesites, which were under water, were sold to New Yorkers yearning for sunshine, and if somebody didn't make a fortune selling horse urine as a cancer cure, it wasn't because of government restrictions—it was because there were so many other ways to get rich.

* * *

I really didn't know much about the way a bank operated until a bank was help up and robbed in a small town called Quincy in the north central part of Washington state. Quincy was about 30 miles from Wenatchee. I was working on a newspaper in 1932 when the holdup occurred.

The bandits were located a couple of weeks later

in the southwest part of Washington, and I, covering the police and sheriff's departments for the paper, accompanied Sheriff Nelson and Police Chief Evans to Vancouver. I remember well the occasion and the movie-style arrest of the bank robbers because I was nearly killed while trying to find a safe place from which to observe the arrest. In the cellar soil, in the house that the bandits had temporarily rented, we found about ten or twelve glass jars filled with the money they had taken from the bank, along with a large black cash box, the sort in which business offices often kept postage stamps and small amounts of money.

Upon our return from Vancouver, I was also in the sheriff's office when the bank people came to identify the bandits and the money. What surprised me was their reaction. They seemed much more interested in the black cash box than in the more than three thousand dollars we had brought back with the prisoners, and they were visibly disappointed when told they could not take the black box with them before the trial of the bandits. What really jolted me, however, was the discovery that the black box did not contain postage stamps and small change. It contained notes and mortgages totaling more than a quarter of a million dollars.

To say I was surprised would be an understatement. How could the bank's owners who had, as I learned, invested only $20,000 of their own money in opening the bank, now collect interest on a quarter of a million dollars? Well, I might have put that mystery away, along with the many others for which I had not yet been able to find answers, were it not for something else that happened in 1932 when the

Great Depression was at its worst. It was an item that appeared in many newspapers—including the one on which I worked—about a traveling salesman. Stories about traveling salesmen were always good for a laugh, because they were always off-color jokes about the way they seduced farmers' daughters. You know the kind:

"Did you hear the one about the farmer's daughter who was seduced by a traveling salesman and she began to cry and said, 'My parents told me again and again to stay away from traveling salesmen, and here I let you overwhelm me and in less than thirty minutes I am seduced twice.' And the salesman says: 'What do you mean you're seduced twice, it was only once,' and she gets real mad and screams, 'Are you telling me, you bastard, that that's all there is, that you're through?'" This next story, however, appeared in the newspapers because it was timely. It dealt with the way money works.

The traveling salesman gave a hotel owner a ten dollar bill for use of a room and meals in the hotel's dining room. The hotel owner used the bill to pay the meat market, which provided food for the dining room. The market owner used it to pay the farmer who provided the large side of beef. The farmer used it to pay his hired hand, who, in turn, decided to get married and pay the preacher with the bill. The preacher bought a pair of shoes with the bill. The shoe store owner added the bill to other proceeds from sale of shoes, and took the proceeds to his bank. At the bank the teller informed him that the ten dollar bill was useless; it was a counterfeit bill.

What we learn from this traveling salesman story is that money, legal and counterfeit, is nothing more than a medium for exchanging goods and/or services. And yet, like the biblical lilies of the field, which neither toil nor spin, it is the medium of exchange which determines the conditions and terms of the toiling and spinning. In other words, it becomes the tail that wags the dog.

***

There was a time in human history when medium of exchange devices were not needed. That was called the barter period, when the commodities themselves were traded for each other. This practice, however, was possible only among members of a tribe, or with friendly nearby tribes. But the barter period ended when traveling increased and more and more new commodities from distant lands became available. The search then began for a commodity which everyone would be willing to trade for what they had, even if they didn't need it. Everyone would accept the commodity because of its scarcity, and the certainty it would be accepted by others in trade for what they did need.

Many centuries passed before gold became a medium of exchange, with silver following later. Egyptian hieroglyphics reveal gold's existence more than five thousand years before the birth of Christ, although its discovery near watercourses goes back to the prehistoric eras when primitive man lived near them, and must surely have been attracted to the shiny nuggets. Many other commodities were tried before, to use a newspaper cliche, gold got the nod, including cattle. The English word "pecuniary" reflects that period in history, for it means "anything that is related to money," and comes from the Latin word "pecus," cattle.

With the above as a background, we can now talk about the circumstances leading to several people in Quincy, Washington investing $20,000 in the ownership of a bank and collecting interest on more than a quarter million dollars.

***

Among the most important consequences of gold's acceptance as a medium for exchanging commodities was the prestige it created for goldsmiths. This was not so much because the goldsmiths fashioned crowns for kings and other rulers, as well as decorations for worship temples and gold coins. It was for an entirely different reason. It was because murderous highwaymen infected all the roads, and the only place where gold was safe was in the specially built, constantly-guarded vaults in the shops of the goldsmiths.

Goldsmiths also then became gold keepers. Thus, a new enterprise came into existence. When owners brought gold to the goldsmith/keepers, the keepers, after setting aside a portion of the gold for themselves, gave the owners receipts for the balance. The gold owners were not long in discovering they did not need to make trips to the vaults. The receipts, signed by the goldsmith/keepers, men of such high repute, were accepted in lieu of the gold itself. The gold owners soon began to ask for six one-ounce receipts instead of one six-ounce receipt. From then on, whoever held the receipt notes became the gold's owner.

Meanwhile, the goldsmith/keepers were trying to figure out what to do with the gold itself. It remained the most important part of the medium of exchange process, but it was no longer used for that purpose. Only if each gold owner suddenly decided, for whatever reason, that he wanted to turn in his receipt notes for gold, would the goldsmith/keepers need all of it. So, making certain that there would always be enough gold available to take care of those who might want to turn in their receipt notes, the goldsmith/keepers began to provide notes to trustworthy individuals in the way they always provided them to gold owners. Those who accepted the notes promised to return an equal number at a specified date, plus a number of additional notes for the goldsmith/keepers who had trusted them.

And that kind of a transaction is called CREDIT, for the word comes from the Latin word that means "trust." It means providing somebody with exchange notes (in whatever form) and trusting him to return a similar number at a given time, plus a few additional ones for the provider.

***

A modern commercial bank operates like a goldsmith/keeper did, but with a great many elaborations. Modern bankers don't "trust." They are like the lady who was seven months pregnant and somebody said, "I see you're expecting." She says, "I'm not expecting, I know damned well what's going to happen."

There used to be a story about a one-eyed banker that went something like this:

"How can you tell which is the glass eye and which is the real eye?"

"The glass eye seems to be a little softer and more

friendly than the real eye."

A modern banker doesn't "trust." He works by the book and knows damned well what's going to happen. Money, to be sure, carries the words "In God We Trust." But that, I submit, may be a bit blasphemous, considering what Jesus had to say about mammon, the god of money and greed. The New Testament quotes Him in Matthew 6:24: "No man can serve two masters: For either he will hate the one, and love the other; or else he will hold to the one and despise the other. Ye cannot serve God and Mammon."

To many Christians, the god of money may appear as a mythical subject, but to Jesus, I think, mammon was as much a symbol of money and greed, as money is a symbol of property ownership today. Jesus was also a prophet.

Look what thirty pieces of silver did for Him. Moreover, "In God We Trust" began to appear on paper money only in 1962 when we seemed to have nobody else we could trust. The nation was still reeling from the McCarthy-created mass hysteria, which also forced us to add the word "under God" to the Pledge of Allegiance.

Those were the days in Hollywood, how well I remember them, when the wife of a writer or actor, who wanted to buy a chicken, had to ask for one that didn't have a left wing.

Anyway, for practical purposes, a banker might say: "O.K. In God We Trust, but mister, if you want action, you better sign on the dotted line.

If God really needs a loan we'll give it serious consideration."

***

Let us begin the dotted line signing, not by seeking a loan from a bank, but by depositing our hundred dollar paycheck. We affix our name on the back of the check and hand it to a bank teller. We can have it recorded in a checking account or in a savings account. Both are called "demand deposits." The difference is that in the "savings account" we may have to notify the bank in advance if we play to "demand" all, or a part of, our money, and in a checking account we do not have to do that.

What happens next is this: The part of the money, the balance, that remains in the bank after checks have been cashed, or withdrawn from the savings account, becomes a bank "asset," in the sense that the money can be used for loans by the bank to others, or otherwise invested. (Before the Federal Deposit Insurance Corporation was created, banks were not allowed to use ALL of the deposits as "assets" for loans or investments. They had to create "liquidity reserves," more or less, the way the goldsmith/keepers made sure enough gold was always on hand to exchange for the notes.) In any event, we are compensated when the bank pays us interest on our savings account deposits and the right to pay our bills with checks from our checking account. Quite recently, banks were given permission to pay interest also for checking accounts in order to increase deposits.

***

Why the great need for deposits? Listen to what the thirtieth president of the United States, Calvin "Silent Cal" Coolidge, had to say:

"The business of business is business." Equally clear

was his answer when asked for an opinion on whether our World War One allies should be forced to pay back the loans we made to them during the war. "They hired the money, didn't they?" said the president. "Silent Cal" was always very cautious about making commitments. On one occasion his private train was traveling through Montana, and a member of his cabinet traveling with him pointed to a dozen or more white sheep grazing on a sloping hillside and asked: "Mr. President, do not those white sheep against the green hills make a wonderful scene?" The president surveyed the pastoral scene and said: "Well, they certainly look white on this side." Without deposits there would not have been any business for President Coolidge to comment on, and without banks and credit, anarchy would surely prevail.

***

In the Bank Business, bank balances build bigger buck balances. This silly alliteration is, however, exactly what happens in the creation of credit by commercial banks. We already knew that whatever the amount of our balance from the hundred dollar paycheck we deposited in the bank, it became a bank "asset," which the bank could loan or invest. But there was no profit for the bank in that transaction, was there? As a matter of fact, the bank lost money when it paid interest and provided services, such as handling our checks.

The profits, however, begin to flow when the deposit balances create enough "assets" for the bank's loan and investment department to get into the act. When OPEN FOR BUSINESS signs appear over the doors of these departments, the above silly alliteration becomes a reality. Loans and investments are obvious "assets" and the credit created from these sources is the real reason banks are in business, because here they're dealing with real big bucks.

***

Let us imagine we're going to the bank again, this time not to deposit a hundred dollars, but to borrow that sum. We answer all the questions correctly, sign on the dotted line in several places, and arrange for the loan's repayment. What happens is this: Except for the repayment provision, the loan transaction is an encore of the deposit scenario. The banker doesn't give us the money. He deposits it in his bank for us, and gives us a checkbook. The money is recorded in the bank's deposit columns, and as such it also appears in the bank's "assets" columns. It is easy to see what that means. It means that loans and investments by commercial banks increase their "assets," and therefore their potential for creating credit at an ever-increasing rate.

Is that good or bad? Remember the Great Depression and the speculators who ran wild because credit was so easily available. The United States Constitution requires Congress "to coin money, regulate the value thereof, and fix the standard of weights and measures." Whether WE THE PEOPLE, in order to form a more perfect union, were wise in turning this crucial chore over to Congress, which turned it over to bankers, or whether we're getting what we deserve, is something in which I don't want to become involved.

***

Are there credit cards in heaven? The purveyors of the cards would have us believe that the cards themselves are a God-inspired way for a civilized society to provided itself with everything it needs to survive, including the purchase of God's divine blessing over television. I strongly disagree. I think that if there is a heaven, it is because the heavenly mailboxes are not filled daily with offers to send additional cards to heaven's inhabitants.

And speaking of heaven and credit cards, let me tell you the story of the two brothers, one of whom was a spendthrift and the other quite wealthy.

The spendthrift worked occasionally, but mostly he depended on his wealthy brother for money. Finally there came a day when the wealthy brother said enough is enough. "I will give you the $200 you asked for," said he to his brother, "but it will have to be a loan at nine percent interest." The spendthrift was shocked. "What would our poor mother in heaven say," he shouted, "if she looked down on us and saw one of her sons demanding nine percent interest for a loan to her other son?"

"If she looks down on us," replied the wealthy one, "it will look like only six percent."

FIDDLER ON THE ROOF

And My Years in Czarist Russia

FIDDLER ON THE ROOF is a play that deals, in an entertaining manner, with a tragic period in the centuries-old struggle of Jews to survive in alien lands.

Based on the stories by an author who lived through those years of anti-Semitic horror, it is a mosaic, a patch-quilt which mirrors the lives of Jews in Russia during the last half of the 19th century and the first decade of the 20th, when anti-Semitism, generated by superstitious priests with the blessing of the czars, was at its worst.

The first thing you will see as the curtain rises on Act One will be a scene that tells you what the play is all about. You will see a small Jewish man in a chair that straddles the ridgepiece of a dilapidated house.

While the chair teeters dangerously, he is playing a plaintive Jewish tune on his fiddle. It symbolizes the precarious life of Jews through the ages.

The play's fictional ghetto, Anatevka, and its inhabitants, might have been any one of the many ghettos that were scattered throughout the Jewish Pale in Russia before the 1917 Revolution. (We will talk about the Pale in a minute.) Anatevka's inhabitants, for instance, were amazingly similar to those of Zemlyanka, the ghetto in which I was born. Anatevka, however, did not have as we did, a large white house at the end of our street, where the "prostitutka" (prostitutes) lived, and where soldiers came twice a month, when they got paid and got drunk and we children had to stay indoors all day.

My own Uncle Nochem did not resemble Tevye

the milkman physically. But Uncle Nochem was a milkman, and talked frequently with Jehovah on an intimate man-to-God basis, just as Tevye did. Sometimes as his horse plodded along in the predawn silence, Uncle Nochem recited the Psalms. (The "ch" in names such as Uncle Nochem, by the way, is pronounced as you would "kh" with the tip of your tongue near the roof of your mouth without touching it.)

If you look at a map of the European part of the Soviet Union you will find the Ukrainian Soviet Socialist Republic in the southwest corner, and Kiev, its capital, roughly in the center. About 25 miles below Kiev you will see in tiny letters a place called Pereyaslavl. That's where the author of the short stories was born in 1859. During the circumcision ritual he was named Solomon Rabinowitz. He became known throughout the world as Sholem Aleichem, and in America, where he died in 1916, as the Jewish Mark Twain.

In selecting the pseudonym Sholem Aleichem— "peace be unto you," the words Jews use when greeting each other—he was expressing a hope for a better future. For hope was what Jews lived on. The Passover ritual always ended with a toast: "L'shono haboh v' Yerushelayem"—next year in Jerusalem— and my mother was sure than when the Messiah came he would see to it that we Jews would return to our homeland, on rafts as thin as cigarette paper, and all the gentiles in their boats would drown.

Well, about 75 miles above Kiev you will see a place called Chernigov.

Zemlyanka, the ghetto that was my birthplace, 28 years after the birth of Sholem Aleichem, was on the outskirts of Chernigov. Both ghettos were inside the Jewish Pale.

A pale, briefly, is a land area enclosed by real or imaginary stakes.

The Jewish Pale was a large area that ran along the western Russian border, with the Black Sea on the south and the Baltic Sea on the north.

It was created in the early 1700's by Catherine the Second, who is also known as Catherine the Great, during the partitioning of Poland among Russia, Austria and Prussia. Catherine, as most Russian histories will tell you, was the empress with a restless libido, who had love affairs with nearly all her cabinet ministers. The most important was Grigori Potemkin, universally recognized as having been one of Europe's most influential diplomats in the 18th century. What triggered creation of the pale was the fact that the portion of Poland that became Russia was home for nearly all of Poland's Jewish population at that time, and Catherine had nightmares of Polish Jews and Russian Jews flooding Russia and expanding eastward.

Life for Russian Jews was always precarious. With creation of the pale new restrictions were constantly being added. Jews could not own property in rural areas, and if they ran a business it was rigidly controlled. All the inhabitants could be, and were, frequently, evicted from their ghetto homes en masse and without warning.

There was a twenty-six year respite for Jews during the reign of Alexander the Second—a humane czar by czarist standards—from 1855 to 1881. He had freed the Russian serfs eighteen months before President Lincoln's Emancipation Proclamation, and was assassinated as was the American president.

Czar Alexander not only ended many of the rigid

restrictions on Jews, but also compensated some of the descendants of those who had been victims of atrocities, among whom were people who had been kidnapped as children and dragged off to be raised as soldiers for the czars. These were allowed to live anywhere they wished and to engage in any enterprise of their choosing.

They had other benefits unavailable to most Jews. And many became wealthy.

(One such family with 16 children lived in Chernigov. A daughter named Angelika Balabanova became an associate of Benito Mussolini in the publication of the socialist newspaper Avanti, before he became Italy's dictator. She became one of the many activists in the Bolshevik revolution who were disillusioned.)

***

There was a big difference between the assassin who took President Lincoln's life, and the five men involved in the assassination of Czar Alexander. The latter were nihilists.

Nihilism was a libertarian movement whose members were mostly intellectuals. They believed in complete freedom of the individual from governments, as well as moral and religious restrictions. They believed that only reason and science should be used in solving social and other problems, and that this could be achieved only by a cultured minority in control. And, I might add, a terrible number of assassinations.

Alexander the Third, who succeeded the assassinated czar, blamed the Jews for everything that had happened during his father's reign, including the reforms. Shortly after the murder of his father, on April 29, 1881, he ordered all Jews who had been allowed to live in St. Petersburg—now Leningrad—out of the Russian capital and from other parts of Russia outside of the ghettos. That was when the anti-Semitism reign of terror began, which affected my family, and all other Russian Jews.

The explanations for the upheaval in Russia that ushered in the 20th century were many and varied, but all centered around the ineptitude of Czar Nicholas II, Russia's last czar, to cope with crucial problems. As the century's earliest years passed, government corruption increased, the war with Japan was lost and Lenin's influence began to be felt. And with each crisis came the inevitable anti-Semitic riots.

Most of the riots, especially those of 1905, were described as massacres in whatever records were available. Those that occurred in Poland were the worst. One in Poland's Biolystok was "a savage massacre." Another at Syedelets (now Sieldlie) was "a great massacre of Jews." Lodz, near Warsaw, was "a violent attack on Jews." The one in Kishinev, Rumania, reported 45 Jews killed, 500 injured, 700 homes destroyed. Kiev, Mogiliv, Bobruisk—my father's birthplace—were ravaged by riots.

Here is a short excerpt from a long report of 1905 during which occurred an event that has become known as "Bloody Sunday."

"The country is in upheaval the entire year. Serious trouble occurs on Sunday, January 22, when troops in St. Petersburg fire upon strikers who are marching to the Winter Palace under leadership of Father Gapon to petition the czar for reforms, many hundreds of men, women and children are killed.

The massacre has far-reaching effects at Radom, Vilno, Saratov, Narva, etc.

Prosecutor General Soinien of Finland, is killed February 6, Grand Duke Sergius, uncle of the czar, is assassinated. Terrible massacres of the Jews occur in Odessa and other cities."

Ironically, Father Grigori Capon, who was leading the hymn-singing strikers and their families to the czar's palace, had been asked to do so by the czar's secret police, in an attempt to keep them from joining the movements inspired by the Lenin Bolsheviks.

***

More than 80 years later, I need only to shut my eyes to find myself in my ghetto home and hear the clamor outside punctuated by the muffled cries "baitye zhidi, baitye zhide"—kill the Jews, kill the Jews.

There were ten of us living in our Zemlyanka home on Yaropol'skaya Oolitza ("oolitza" means street in Russian, with the letter "l" pronounced as the two "l"s in million)—my father, mother and grandmother, four older brothers, my younger sister and my youngest brother. It was a large house with an earthen floor and the usual Russian brick and clay oven, which began in one of the corners, and ran about half the length of the wall. There were two smaller rooms, one for my parents, and the other for grandmother.

In the center of the large room was the big square table with an oilcloth which reached to the floor. At sundown Friday, this was replaced by a sparkling white tablecloth for the blessing of the candles and the great meal which ushered in the Sabbath. Near the door leading to the outside was a high bureau, behind which the leather-covered billyclubs that my older brothers used to defend themselves during the pogroms were hidden. My grandmother sits on a bench and is staring vacantly into space. My mother is sitting near her and is mumbling prayers. Suddenly the door crashes open and my two brothers—Shlaimke and Shmuel—rush into the room. There is blood on the right side of Shlaimke's face. They push aside the bureau by the door, grab several home-built billyclubs and run toward the door to join their comrades. My mother is screaming, "gai nit, gai nit"—don't go, don't go.

My poor, long-suffering Jewish mother was terrified at the possibility of injury, even death, for Shlaimke and Shmuel, and, at the same time, worried about God's reaction to what they were doing. Surely, He knew what His plan was. If He wanted the riots stopped, He could achieve that by a snap of His divine fingers. Did He not send an angel to stop the hand of Abraham as he was about to plunge a knife into the heart of his son Isaac?

In FIDDLER ON THE ROOF, you will see counterparts not only of my Uncle Nochem, but by parents and our neighbors and all Jews living inside the pale, about whom Sholem Aleichem wrote. You will see incidents that symbolize the despair and agony of Jewish parents in Russia, when a son or daughter becomes involved with a gentile girl or boy. You will see a growing interest among young people toward radicalism, and with a comparable loss of interest in traditional ways of dealing with anti-Semitism. There are also scenes in which the dialogue is a suggestion by Orthodox Jewish parents that Leviticus, Numbers, Deuteronomy and the Holy Tablets are all young people need for proper behavior and solving anti-Semitism and other conflicts. You will then be hearing an echo of my mother's cry "don't go, don't go."

***

Why has anti-Semitism been so omnipresent for so many centuries? Why does dislike for Jews among so many people range from simply wanting to avoid them to supporting the murder of them? For Russian czars, the Jews were ready-made scapegoats. Everything that happened—whether it was a natural disaster or a blunder by a czar himself—could be blamed on the Jews. Thus the Roman caesars used to give the restive populace circuses to keep it in check, and the czars (which comes from the word caesar) pacified the Russian masses by letting them vent their anger on Jews. In a nation with illiteracy approaching 90 percent, it was not difficult for superstitious priests to create an impression that droughts, floods and other natural disasters were God's way of expressing anger because Russia harbored people who killed His Son, Jesus. Strikes and the growing radicalism among workers, along with other economic dislocations, were blamed on the followers of the Jew Karl Marx. (His father converted to Christianity when Karl was five to avoid persecution.) Jewish bankers were blamed for financial crises. The disappearance of children was blamed on Jews, because, said the rumormongers, Jews needed Christian blood for their Passover ritual. The Jewish religious rite called circumcision became a sadistic mutilation of newborn infants.

The role of Jewish bankers is worth examining because

it remains an issue with regard to today's anti-Semitism, even though banking is today far from a Jewish monopoly. Jews became an important element in the money sector during the years when the church placed rigid restrictions on Catholics, at times forbidding participation of Catholics in money matters entirely. ("Love of money is the root of all evil," warned Paul's favorite disciple Timothy.) But Jews were involved in the money business even before that, for an entirely different reason. Hounded as they were for centuries from one nation to another, they found money in the form of gold and other forms the easiest things to take with them when driven from their homes.

Not surprisingly, the orders to leave often came when loans, to kings and other overlords, became due. I personally know of no better way of clearing up a debt than by getting rid of the creditor, do you?

Outside of Russia, another reason for murderous attacks on Jews surfaced during the years of the devastating Black Death Plague, which killed one-third of the European population. It was observed that fewer Jews died, compared to the thousands of non-Jews who perished in the plague.

The rumors spread throughout Europe that the anti-Christ Jews stole out of their ghettos during the night and poisoned the wells and other water sources.

***

Near the end of November in 1905, after what was described as the "terrible massacre of Jews in Odessa," Sholem Aleichem joined hundreds of others in the exodus of Jews from Russia. The exodus is mirrored in United States official immigration figures: 1902,

1903, 1904, the immigrants arriving total six figures 648,743, 857,046, 812,870. They jump dramatically for the dreadful years 1905, 1906, 1907 to seven figures 1,027,421, 1,100,735, 1,285,349. Then they taper off again, which did not mean an end to the anti-Semitic riots. The figures, of course, represent immigrants from all over the world to America, but the increase during the three years of anti-Semitic riots cannot be attributed to anything other than the exodus of Jews from Russia.

Joining the hundreds who left Russia during those dreadful years was my oldest brother, Nehemia. His destination, however, was Canada, because several of his "Khaveirim"—comrades—were already there. His goal, as was the goal of nearly everyone else, was to start earning money to bring the rest of the family to America. Shortly after his arrival in Canada we received sensational news from him. "Here," wrote Nehemia, "even workers ride to work on bicycles." (Many Jews chose Canada because Moritz Hirsch, a Jewish financier in Germany, founded a $50,000,000 colonization project in Canada, Argentina and elsewhere for persecuted Jews.)

I am able to testify that in 1910, when I, along with the last members of my family, arrived in Winnipeg, that the first thing I saw outside of the Canadian Pacific Railway depot were a lot of people riding bicycles. Soon, I was no longer called a "vshiei zhid"— a lousy Jew. I was called a "sheeny" or a "kike" or a "fucking Jew." There were no streets paved with gold anywhere, and my father, who was a harnessmaker in Russia, along with many other bearded Orthodox Jews, could not find jobs because they would not work on the Sabbath. Many became pushcart peddlers, then small merchants, then large merchants. If you have been wondering why so many large department stores have Jewish owners, and why Jews are bankers and on boards of giant corporations, you now have the answer. If I were not an agnostic and believed in miracles, I would say Jehovah did it deliberately.

***

Sholem Aleichem wrote in Hebrew, the language of today's Israel and of the Old Testament. He also wrote in Russian. But the short stories on which FIDDLER ON THE ROOF is based were written in Yiddish, for only Yiddish, with its great accumulation of idioms, could give expression to the bittersweet humor of the stories. At the risk of being considered biased, subjective, parochial—I submit that Yiddish is the world's most colorful language.

Why, you may ask, do the Germans speak German, the French French, the Spanish Spanish, the Russians Russian, but Jews don't speak Jewish...they speak Yiddish, why? Well, it happened this way; the word Jew comes from Judean, a member of an ancient tribe of Israelites who lived in Babylonia, then part of what is now Iraq. About five centuries before the birth of Christ, they were driven from Babylonia. And later—between the 10th and 13th centuries after the birth of Christ, finds them living in miserable ghettos along the Rhine River in Germany.

Here, along the Rhine, the Jews had company—ghettos filled with refugees from the fury of the highly-romanticized Crusaders, who, in their search for the tomb of Jesus, slaughtered thousands of muslims along with the hundreds of Jews and other non-believers.

Praise the Lord! Thus developed a colorful, a sort of super-language dominated by the Jewish and German languages—Judisch (Jewish) and Teutsch (German)—Judisch-Teutsch became Yiddish. Before Yiddish became a universal language for Jews, they of course spoke Hebrew, the origin of which seems to be buried in antiquity.

What is known is that it was one of the Semitic languages used by the people who inhabited what the bible calls "the land of Canaan" along the eastern coast of the Mediterranean. When Israel made Hebrew its official language upon becoming a nation in 1948, the Israelis faced a language problem.

There were obviously no Hebrew words for a good many things which were nonexistent prior to the 20th century. So a "computer" became a "mahshev," the Hebrew word for a "thinker," and "unemployment" became "avtalah," the Hebrew word for "nonexistent."

Other nations have had occasions when it became necessary to create new words. In Russia, for instance, Catherine the Great, herself of German origin, arranged for thousands of Germans to become farmers and convert the Ukraine into what became "Europe's Bread Basket." They could not communicate with the Russians, they could only gesticulate with their hands.

The Russians called them "dumb idiots." So the Russian word for a German is "nemetz," from the Russian adjective "nemoi" which means "dumb." And if you're not an etymology student, you may be interested in knowing that a bolt with the thread on the outside is called the male part and the nut with the thread inside is the female part. You can read

about it in the Encyclopedia Americana under the
word "screw" and in Webster's large dictionary under "thread." I keep nuts and bolts on the work bench
in my garage in containers marked "His" and "Hers."

***

Yiddish, as I said, is the world's most colorful language,
for no other language can equal it as a language to
which so many others have contributed during the
centuries when Jews were harassed and driven from
one part of the world to another. What adds color
to a language is its idioms; that is, words and phrases
which become part of the language with the passage of time to accommodate changes in environment and lifestyle. They are non- transferable from
one language to another. One man's speech is another man's gibberish. "Hogwash," "skullduggery,"
"sleazy," "porkbarrel," and thousands of other American
idioms mean nothing to people in other parts of the
world.

Aphorisms have always been particularly apt and
effective. If you asked my Jewish mother whether
praying for the czar would help the Jews or not,
she would shake her head and say firmly: "Ess vet
helfen vee a tainten kaunes." (It will help the way
enemas will help a dead man.) We needed no doctors in Russia. Enemas and chicken soup took care
of everything that ails mankind. Chutzpah, which
means temerity or audacity, and was once applied
to those who questioned the wisdom of God, now
applies to someone who asks you for a cigarette and
gets mad when you give him one that isn't the kind
he smokes. That's real chutzpah.

What intrigues me about Sholem Aleichem's stories is that the characters in them are not fictional—they portray real people and their relationship to each other and to God. As a matter of fact, had tape recorders been available and you could have heard my father and mother talking, you would say that's FIDDLER ON THE ROOF'S "mama and papa" talking.

"Every time we move to another house," complains my mother, "I have trouble sleeping the first two or three nights."

"So why don't you sleep somewhere else the first two or three nights?" asks my father.

I can see my mother now. She looks puzzled. It takes a minute or two to figure out what's wrong with the advice. Then she looks at the ceiling and addresses God: "What have I done, Gottenue, to deserve such an apikoros?"—(a free thinker).

Actually my father was very religious. He was meticulous in his observance of all Orthodox rituals, and rated high in disputations with other Jews on the Talmud, the compilation of all Hebrew civil and canonical laws. What caused my mother to call him an "apikoros" was his tendency to lean toward Hasidism, a movement that originated in Poland in the 18th century, which puts emphasis on contemplation and worship rather than dogma and ritual.

It was, as a matter of fact, this mild impiety which forced him to become a harnessmaker. You see, he originally earned a livelihood by constructing phylacteries, "tfilim"—those small, leather-covered square boxes Orthodox Jews wear when praying. Each has two long narrow strips of leather trailing from them. One is placed on the forehead, the other wound around the left arm. Inside each, father would place a small piece of parchment on which he had inscribed in tiny letters passages from Exodus and Deuteronomy. When rumors began to spread that my father was not an unblemished pious Jew and that he had been heard to say things bordering on impiety, he began to lose customers. He then turned to harnessmaking.

"Horses," he said, "don't care who makes the harness, which they don't like anyway."

***

I do not know where the stories came from that my father used to tell us while we were still in Russia. He was born in 1860, during the early years of the reign of the reform czar, Alexander II. That was a year after Sholem Aleichem was born and several years after another great Yiddish humorist, Isaac Leibush Peretz, appeared. In any event, the stories by both Sholem Aleichem and Peretz were circulating in Jewish ghettos by the time I was six or seven, and my father may have been simply relating them to us, or as an expert at hyperbolizing, may have made them up for our benefit. One I recall concerned a champion liar telling his friends about a merchant who had to make a trip in his sled over the steppes to a place many miles away.

As he was driving along he suddenly saw that a pack of wolves had begun to follow the sled. He counted thirty wolves, and knowing something about the way wolves lived, he took his gun and shot the biggest one. Sure enough, the rest of the pack stopped to devour the one that was shot. When they resumed their chase and came near the sled, the merchant shot another, and so on and so on, until only one wolf was left.

"Hey, wait a minute," said one of the listeners, "do you mean to tell us that the one wolf had the other 29 wolves inside him?"

"Well," said the champion liar, "come to think of it, he was wobbling a little as he ran."

We all laughed because in Yiddish the word used to describe "wobbling" is "Katzet'zach," which is one of those wonderful Yiddish words creating a mental picture of a drunken duck trying to run.

***

"When, at the age of seven, I asked my father why I could not commit sins before my Bar Mitzvah at thirteen, when boys become responsible for their sins, he patted me on the head and replied: "My son, when a sin is committed, God has to blame somebody. If it's not you, it's me. And I've got so many of my own. Just be a good boy, please."

I learned a great deal about Jewish history from my brother, Shmuel, who talked to me about the Magidim—the plural for Magid, about whom very little appears to have been said anywhere. (In the New Testament they are called the Magis, the wise men. The Magis were also an ancient Persian priestly caste.) The Jewish Magidim had for centuries been roving preachers. They used to turn up in Chernigov, said Shmuel, a crowd would gather about them and they would talk about the Hebrew prophets. They asked for little more than food and a place to sleep. But when Theodore Herzl launched the Zionist movement in the middle of the 19th century, and a crusade for a Jewish homeland got under way in earnest, many Magidim began to talk about the future as well as the past.

When he was about fifteen years old, a Magid gathered the people around him, and this is what he said: "We must make certain that in building a homeland, it is without those evils which have made it possible for those, who do not believe as we do, to persecute us. For those who have practiced persecution of Jews are not the only ones who are able to hate and be prejudiced and practice exploitation. We must not build a homeland where those who do not labor live in comfort and many who do labor go hungry."

When the time came for Shmuel and his comrades, who had originally organized to battle anti-Semitic rioters, to become active in the crusade for a Jewish homeland, they became Poale-Zionists—worker-Zionists—who favored making a homeland a socialist state.

***

Only Orthodox Jews dreamed of a Messiah returning them to their ancient homeland. Theodor Herzl, the founder of Zionism, and his followers, had no illusions. The Turks made it clear that Palestine was "off limits" to Jews.

In his diaries, the Jewish leader tells of a meeting with the British Prime Minister Gladstone while searching for a homeland. Gladstone unrolled a huge wall map showing the mighty British Empire, and with a long wooden pointer began roaming over the map. It reminded him, wrote Herzl, of the owner of a cluttered shop searching for something a customer needs and saying, "Wait, wait, I know it's here someplace."

Not until the Turks lost Arabia as a consequence of their partnership with Germany in World War One did a Palestine homeland for Jews become a possibility, and the chance arose most unusually. About eighteen months before the war ended, Czar Nicholas abdicated. The struggle for control of Russia was between Kerensky's menshiviks, who wanted to stay in the war, and Lenin and Trotsky's bolsheviks, who didn't. Both had Jews in high places, notably Trotsky who was himself a Jew. The mountain decided to go to Mahomet. Jews suddenly became very popular.

That was in 1917, which was also the year the famous carefully worded Balfour Declaration was issued. It merely said that the British looked favorably on a Jewish homeland in Palestine. But it was enough to set off unprecedented riots—secretly supported by the British Colonial Office—riots which might as well have brought on the biblical Armageddon.

Shmuel fled Russia because of his political activities. On a spring day in 1908 that was so pleasant the front door could be kept open, I saw three policemen approach the house (the sight of a "gordovoi," the Russian word for policeman, always made me tremble with fear). They came in and asked for Shmuel, who was not at home. Then they made a quick search of the house, not touching, for some reason, the bureau by the door behind which were hidden three of the leather-covered billyclubs. They then ordered my father to go with them to the harness shop in downtown Chernigov. When Shmuel came home and learned what had happened, he kissed my mother and grandmother, who were both sobbing and praying, and the rest of us, and hurried away to Uncle Nochem's where a hiding place had been prepared for just such a contingency. He feared most that the police would find the dozen or so billyclubs that were hidden on a shelf in the back room of father's harness shop. It turned out, however, that they were hunting for a homemade hectograph and inflammatory handbills my brother was reported to have been involved in producing.

These hectographs were simple to make and played an important part in developing revolutionary interest among the Russian masses. Lenin wrote his first important essay on one such hectograph. They were shallow pans filled with a gelatin substance. A message was written on a carbon-coated piece of paper and then pressed against the gelatin. From the impression it was possible to produce hundreds of copies of the message. The policemen found no hectographs or any handbills, and did not look for billyclubs. They let my father go after warning him of what could happen to parents who raise children who become troublemakers.

***

Chernigov, in sharp contrast to bleak Kordovka, was a magnificent city.

It was all but destroyed during World War II, first by the retreating Red Army's "scorched earth" policy as the Nazis drew near, and then by the Nazis as the Red Army rebounded. But one of the great structures that both sides left untouched was the Cathedral of the Savior in the heart of downtown Chernigov. To this day, the Cathedral of the Savior remains among

Russia's oldest, and one of the world's most famous monuments of Slavic art. Built in the Byzantine style, work on it began shortly after 955 A.D., when Princess Olga of Kiev became a Christian, and was completed in 1040 A.D.

One onerous day, when I was mad at God for not doing something to the drunken soldiers who forced us to stay indoors all day, I decided to defy Him as I was passing the Cathedral, and so did not spit on the sidewalk to ward off the "evil eye" as my mother always did. I demonstrated my "chutzpah" by deliberately walking toward the huge sculpted doors and glancing inside the empty place. And what a sight that was! I held my breath as I saw the many bright colors on the walls and ceiling—red, green yellow, and blue—the hundreds of tall thick candles in huge silver candlesticks the like of which I had never dreamed of, statues, gold icons, more statues and more icons, and the incredibly beautiful stained-glass windows, which filtered the sunlight, making eerie patterns of the shadows of the outside tree branches along the high, hand-carved backs of the empty pews. "Chutzpah" or no "chutzpah," I was frightened, and hardly breathed until I was out of sight of the Cathedral.

Suddenly I realized what a terrible sin I had committed—those stained windows with their beautiful pictures showing men with long hair and flowing robes, holding in their hands long walking sticks with curved ends, and the lady with the naked baby on her lap—they were Christian saints and shepherds—and the lady was the Virgin Mary, and the baby was none other than THEIR God Jesus. What is going to happen to terrible sinners like me?

It was this event that prompted me to pose the

question about pre-Bar Mitzvah sins to my father, and it was his reply that set me on the road to agnosticism. I did not like the idea of my gentle father being forced by God to bear my sins.

***

Mixed in with all the horrors that marked my childhood in czarist Russia, there are other pleasant recollections. I remember so well the many hours I spent in Chernigov's beautiful park, at that time called the "Vaal," watching the Desna River, so far below that the men with long ropes over their shoulders on both sides of the river, pulling loaded barges, looked like dolls. "Vaal" is the Russian word for rampart or fortification and one of my brothers told me that the "Vaal" was the place from which soldiers defended Chernigov many years ago against Tartars and other enemies, who came from up and down the Desna River to try and capture the city. One of the men in charge of the defenders was an adventurous Scotsman with an odd-shaped nose. He became a sort of a folk hero of the Ukraine and is known in history as "Krivonos," which means crooked nose.

When I had a kopek or two, I would buy "kvas," a refreshing drink made from black fermented bread, from a man with a wagon toting pitchers of it.

In the center of the "Vaal" was a space with a lot of benches and a large white screen, and one evening my brother Shlaimke brought me there to sit on the benches with other people. When it became dark, I suddenly heard a whirring noise and when I looked around I saw a patch of bright white light coming from a small square hole of a little house on stilts. The patch of white got wider and wider and when I turned my head again it completely covered the screen. And then wonder of wonders! I saw on the screen a mountain from the top of which came smoke and fire and people were running in every direction. "That's a motion picture," said Shlaimke, delighted at my amazement. "It's called 'The Burning of Pompei'."

***

If you are interested in Sholem Aleichem, you will, I am sure, also be interested in my brother Shlaimke (Sam), for it was from him that I learned, when I was about six years old, that "Sholem Aleichem" was more than something Jews said to each other—it was also the name of a great writer of Yiddish stories. My mother nicknamed him "der Tzigainer," the gypsy, and he really qualified for the nickname. He had swarthy features, did not need pomade for his shiny black hair, and his eyes were those of Moses in my father's bible, the Moses who came down the mountain clutching the holy tablets and let the cavorting drunken Hebrews know what was going to happen to them on Judgment Day. Even before Shlaimke left Russia with father, a year or so before the rest of us left in 1910, he knew all about the founding of the Yiddish theater in Rumania in 1976 by Abraham Goldfaden, and could talk about the early Jewish folk singers who sermonized as they entertained. It did not take Shlaimke long to become involved in the Yiddish theater in Winnipeg , and for the Queens Theater on Selkirk Avenue to become a home away from home. We soon began to

hear names of Yiddish actors in New York, Philadelphia, and Chicago—names, I recall...Jacob Alder,
David Kessler and Boris Tomashevsky.

My own interest in Sholem Aleichem and the Yiddish theater heightened when I appeared in a show
at the Queens Theater. In one scene there was an
anti-Semitic riot, and I was to be one of the children
of families attacked by the rioters. How well I remember my premier appearance in the role of a thespian.
There were about twenty of us. We followed instructions.
We began muttering and shuffling around about half
a minute before the curtain went up. A long sheet
of tin hung from the ceiling by the wall, where it
could not be seen by the audience. When a man shook
it from the bottom it sounded like thunder. As the
curtain rose our muttering became shouts, I forgot
my lines, as did most of the children, and I yelled
the names of everyone in the family. We grabbed
each other as if we were wrestling. The thunder became louder and louder, firecrackers exploded and
colored fires flared up and died away. I was apparently a great success. Clara, Shlaimke's girlfriend at
that time, said my hair looked just like my brother's.
Then she put her arms around me, lifted me from
the floor and pressed me to her bosomy chest and
gave me a long, wet kiss. I felt a troubled tingling
in the lower part of my body. Except for my mother,
this was my first encounter with the opposite sex.

   ***

Coincidentally, with his interest in Yiddish theater, Shlaimke became a dedicated Zionist. In retrospect, I now realize that his dedication reached a

point of zealousness. While I was struggling with the inconsistencies of the English language, (the plural of book is books, but you add an "e" for the plural of ax, and the plural of ox is not oxes, it is oxen, the plural of mouse is mice, while sheep remain sheep), Shlaimke warned me about Shakespeare and Charles Dickens. He accused them of being anti-Semitic for creating despicable Jewish characters such as Shylock in "Merchant of Venice" and Fagin in "Oliver Twist."

My brother murdered the English language. In reporting to Sarah, his wife, that a woman friend had been told by a psychiatrist that she was frustrated, he said: "The doctor said Rose doesn't have a husband so she is defrosted." And our Uncle David from Milwaukee lived near Lake "Mishugen," the Yiddish word for crazy. But with Yiddish he was a miracle worker. He spoke normally as if he was narrating a soliloquy in a dramatic stage production. If he said, "Yes, I will have another bagel," and you didn't understand Yiddish, I am certain you would think you were listening to John Barrymore's "Now is the winter of our discontent" from Richard III.

It was this talent for dramatizing what he had to say that made him an important element in rallying Western Canadian Jewish support for Israel during its struggle to become a nation. He became a full-time lecturer and popular after-dinner speaker on behalf of the cause. Shlaimke died in 1975.

The last time I talked with him face to face was in 1962 when I made a surprise visit to Winnipeg. My sister Anne called what members of the Greene family were still around for a mini-reception in my honor, and, as we used to say, "a good time was had by all." Shlaimke welcomed me as though he was auditioning for a role in Macbeth—"We welcome our brother from California where the sun shines eternally..." We reminisced about the past, recalling only the pleasant events. Nature seems to arrange for painful experiences to diminish from memory with the passage of time.

I am sure Shlaimke would have liked the Yiddish story a Seattle friend told me a couple of years ago, in which humor and pathos combined as they do in so many Yiddish stories.

A wise rabbi—all rabbis in Yiddish stories are "wise"—is talking to a crowd of Jews about God's absolute and non-debatable perfection.

Everything God has created must be perfect. It cannot be otherwise, for God Himself is the ultimate, the supreme example of perfection, and perfection cannot possibly create imperfection. Among the listeners is a poor, bedraggled hunchback. He shuffles forward, a pathetic sight. Now he is before the rabbi. The rabbi appraises him—you can't even say the rabbi is appraising him up and down, for the poor, half-blind hunchback is no more than four-and-a-half feet tall. The hunchback raises his head and speaks:

"Rabbi, look at me...rabbi, look at me and tell me, am I perfect?" The rabbi is silent, then he speaks: "Yes, my son, be of comfort, and praise God, for among hunchbacks you are without doubt the most perfect hunchback in the world."

If you're laughing, shame on you.

THE UBIQUITOUS ISSUE: ABORTION

How It Was a Half Century Ago

(A 1951 letter from me to Anna Roosevelt*)

Dear Anna:

I am sending a copy of a draft for the abortion story you suggested in your letter. It is based on my own research and the material you had sent along with your request. I have not provided a title, but in view of the humane way Denmark has taken care to assure the legitimacy of children born to unmarried mothers, and the help provided pregnant women to avoid abortions, how about, "THERE ARE NO BASTARDS IN DENMARK."

And by the way, Anna, among the material you sent, I found some handwritten notes which seem to reflect your father's fear. I was particularly struck by the words in one: "Defense, FDR, Churchill, Russian Alliance." And another: "Totalitarian oppression in Europe, thru Pearl Harbor." Does it have anything to do with the Yalta Conference you attended with FDR? Anyhow, let me know if you want me to mail it back to you in Berkeley.

Say hello for me to Johnny. I keep thinking about

---

*I was an associate of Eleanor and Anna Roosevelt in a mother-daughter radio commentary over the American Broadcasting Network. An attack of rheumatic fever forced Anna to give up broadcasting and move to Berkeley in the San Francisco Bay area. In 1950 she asked me to put together an article about the abortion problem for her and Dr. Leo Boyle, with whom she had collaborated on the book, Your Pregnancy. The Johnny mentioned in my letter was her son by her second husband, John Boettiger.

the way the grandson of President Franklin Delano
Roosevelt went from door to door on Creston Road
trying to sell the packages of chewing gum I brought
him on my last visit.

Affectionately,

Bill G.

Ruth heard her name called. After a quick self-
conscious glance around the waiting room, she rose
and followed the nurse through a door into a narrow hallway.

In another minute she was in the tiny office at the
end of the hall, and here, as she faced the doctor
who was to perform the operation, she suddenly felt
uncertain and frightened.

The drugstore clerk who sent her to this doctor
had told her there was no danger. And the doctor
himself had assured her when she came to make
arrangements for the operation that everything was
going to be all right.

Still, she'd read so often in the papers about women
who did not survive.

Then there flashed through Ruth's mind once again
the many problems another baby would bring for
her and Charlie...the bills that would have to be added
to those they were already having such a hard time
paying...the many additional things her two children,
Jerry and Danny, would have to do without...their
small home already so crowded it was hard to find
room for any of them...having to give up her job at
the supermarket...

Ruth bit her lip and shivered slightly while sitting across the desk from the unsmiling doctor. Her hands shook as she reached into her handbag for the $150 in 20's and 10's. The doctor moistened an expert thumb and quickly counted the money. He tossed it into the top drawer of his desk and with a jerk of his head motioned Ruth to follow him into the room adjoining the office.

It was the customary doctor's room with the usual equipment. A cabinet with shiny surgical instruments, a sterilizer, an examining table, a sink in one corner, and in another a screen behind which patients could undress and dress. There was also an adjoining recovery room. The nurse pointed to the screen and told Ruth she could undress there.

Two hours later, Ruth, her face pale and her knees shaking, went home in a taxicab. That night she awoke with a dull pain in the pit of her stomach. She took an aspirin and followed this with one of the several tablets the doctor had given her. But the pain did not disappear. It grew worse, and by morning she was in agony.

Frantically, Charlie called a cab and rushed her to General Hospital.

She was given a blood transfusion, large doses of penicillin and other drugs. Ruth died three days later. The coroner's report said death was due to septicemia (blood poisoning), secondary to a perforated uterus and generalized peritonitis.

***

Each year more than one million women in the United States, upon discovering that they are pregnant, "do something" to keep from having babies.

They spend huge sums of money on questionable drugs and paraphernalia in a desperate attempt to avoid becoming a mother. About half of these women, approximately 500,000, go to abortionists to have illegal operations. And each year, it is estimated, between 15,000 and 20,000 die, as Ruth did, from complications that follow these surreptitious visits.

Of those who survive, many suffer irreparable psychological harm, and it is not at all unusual, say psychiatrists, to trace a neurosis in a woman in later years to the work of an abortionist when she was young. The many thousands, who can't afford to pay abortionists, frequently end their pregnancies by deliberate "miscarriages," with the help of pills and other ingenious methods.

There is something dreadfully significant about this desperate determination of one million American women each year to keep pregnancy from following its natural course. They do this despite the fact that it's illegal, despite religious prohibitions, despite moral codes, despite their natural maternal instincts and at the risk of their health, and often pay with their very lives. And yet, notwithstanding the great moral, social and economic implications of this national disgrace at the half-way point of the 20th century, the problem of illegal abortions remains our number one hush- hush problem. It's something people just don't talk about. No editorials are written about it. Radio commentators never comment on it. Magazine articles are hardly ever published dealing with it. Organized women's groups rarely discuss it. Medical societies concern themselves only with those phases which may affect the ethics of their profession.

***

It is a startling and most significant fact that most of the women who seek the help of abortionists are married and many have children at home.

Because there is so little publicity on the subject, there exists a misconception that most of those who go to abortionists are girls and unmarried women. That is not true, and while accurate figures are not available, the best estimates place the number of married women who go to abortionists at anywhere from 60 to 80 percent of the total. This means that each year finds between 300,000 and 400,000 married women in the United States having illegal operations.

***

What prompts women, married or unmarried, to avoid becoming mothers?

There are, of course, many reasons. Poor Ruth's problems symbolize those thousands of other women face today in what Professor Pangloss in Voltaire's "Candide" insisted was "this best of all possible worlds." But the most important reason of all is quite obviously woman's escape from the bedroom and kitchen, where man has assigned her since the beginning of time.

Large families of a half century ago have become the exception and not the rule. And with many states barring abortions completely, and others limiting them to mothers whose lives might be jeopardized, the only alternatives are attempts to end pregnancy with the help of drugs and whatever other means are available. And when these fail there is only the abortionist.

This practitioner may be the regular doctor of medicine who has been expelled from his medical associations for one reason or another. The abortionist may be a nurse, either male or female, who has grasped a smattering of medical know-how from watching doctors work and decides to go into business. Operating, as a rule, in poorly equipped and unsanitary quarters, concerned only with collecting a fee and getting the patient out of the way as quickly as possible, it is amazing that the death toll traceable to illegal abortions is not higher. (Experts in the prosecution of abortionists believe that many doctors, who find a woman they had been called to attend dead from complications of an illegal abortion, record her death from other causes rather than chance becoming involved in an investigation.)

Not all abortionists, of course, operate in dingy, dimly-lit quarters and under unsanitary conditions. The one to whom poor Ruth went had a modest place of business. He was a general practitioner and performed perhaps one or two abortions a week, charging between $100 and $150 for an operation. But there are others who operate in swank offices in exclusive sections of the city and whose fees will run as high as $1,000 for an abortion. Some of these have performed as many as 10 or more such operations a day. At the other extreme are the abortionists who operate in shacks and in trailers and who move from place to place to keep the police from catching up with them. They charge as little as $20 to $25. There isn't any way of knowing how many abortionists operate in this country.

Authorities estimate that the proportion of those caught to those who continue their thriving practice is minuscule. This is because the nature of the business makes it extremely difficult to get evidence to bring about a conviction.

***

So it is, ironically, in Denmark, where Lutheranism is the nation's official religion, that the realities of abortion have been recognized and steps have been taken to cope with its multiple problems. Denmark has set the pace. Back in the 1920's it became obvious to Danish leaders that the country could not go on shutting its eyes and pretending the abortion problem didn't exist. So, in 1925, they launched their social experiment which has since been adopted, with modifications to fit their individual needs, by Sweden, Finland, and Norway.

The Danish program is based on the premise that most abortions can be prevented by an intelligent understanding of the reasons by women want them.

The government of Denmark created an organization known as the Mothers Aid Institute, supported by government funds. Local units of the Institute are scattered all over the country. Each unit is staffed with a social worker, psychiatrist, gynecologist, and a special medical consultant is available when needed. With the establishment of the Institute and its various units, the government began an educational program designed to gain the confidence of women contemplating abortions. The need for saving lives is stressed and everything possible is done to encourage women to make use of the facilities of the various local units of the Institute. At these units, women find sympathetic personnel—people who concentrate on doing everything possible to find out and eliminate problems. The pregnant woman finds government help available for her material problems. Where the woman is unmarried, efforts are made to find her a job and the baby is taken care of until such time as the mother can take care of it herself. The baby is made the legal heir of the father, wherever the father's name is known, and the stigma of illegitimacy is removed.

Briefly, the theory underlying the program is that women basically do not want abortions; they want their babies. And elimination, or at least mitigation, of the reasons why women want abortions will proportionately lessen the number of illegal operations. The program has paid big dividends for the Scandinavian countries that have adopted them. There has been a dramatic drop in abortion death, and most remarkably, a reduction in the number of women who continue wanting to have abortions performed.

Unfortunately not many countries have thought it wise or proper to study the Scandinavian experiment, despite its success. England and the British Commonwealth continue with rigid laws against abortion that have been in effect for centuries, and Germany, Austria, and Japan have laws similar to the British. Western Europe, generally, and South America, where the church hierarchy has the greatest possible influence on the action of lawmakers, have the strongest anti-abortion laws anywhere in the world. But the best information available would appear to indicate that these laws have, if anything, aggravated the problem, and a thriving illegal abortion racket continues in all of these countries.

***

It was inevitable that everything everywhere should change with the end of World War One. Millions were killed, millions more were wounded, and countless orphans wandered throughout Europe. America's customary boisterousness, restrained by the war, exploded in the "Roaring Twenties," during which behavior patterns, which usually develop and change slowly over years, became effective almost overnight. Morals dipped as dress hems rose.

Corset ads began to be replaced by ads for sheer hose in the slick magazines. The shimmy and Charleston replaced the fox trot and slow waltz, elaborate hairdos became bobbed hair. Some women even discovered they could smoke cigarettes in public without being considered prostitutes. But so much has been written about the "Roaring Twenties" there is little left to say that would not be repetitious.

It must be noted, however, that while lifestyles changed radically, laws remained unchanged. Contraceptives, for instance, remained illegal in some states, and in those where they were allowed, the condoms carried a warning that they were to be used "for prevention of venereal disease only."

One did not become aware, however, of the warning until the condom was unrolled and the tiny letters became visible just below the rim of the opening. By that time, if you'll pardon the pun, neither snow, nor rain, nor gloom of night could stop the male.

***

The "Roaring Twenties" collapsed like a skyscraper in a mighty earthquake on October 29, 1929, triggering the nation's worst depression in history and worldwide repercussions. Ironically, two other historically- devastating events followed, each a decade from the other.

1939: September 1—Hitler's Nazis invade Poland,

forcing Britain and France to declare World War Two against Germany and the United States against Japan two years later.

1949: September 23—United States loses the atom bomb monopoly with an announcement by President Truman that the Soviet Union has exploded its own nuclear device. Only two years earlier, Congress approved a $400 million request from Truman to keep communism from spreading into Turkey and Greece. The gloom-and-doom prophets predict an atom bomb race.

From January 16, 1920, when the anti-liquor amendment to the constitution became effective, until the early days of the New Deal in 1933, when the amendment was repealed, the most profitable illicit racket in America was bootlegging. After repeal, the abortionists claimed the bootleggers' position. It was "business as usual" for them, for there was no great outcry by any responsible group for lifting restrictions on abortion as there had been for alcoholic beverages and other forms of human behavior. And it is "business as usual" for the abortionists today, while thousands of women continue agonizing over decisions involving life or death.

No so, however, with another once equally-proscribed subject, which, fortunately, does not have the same heavy religious implications abortion has. The subject is venereal disease, which if discussed at all, used to be identified as a "social disease." A French playwright named Eugene Brieux horrified the censors in France, England, and the United States with a play about a member of French high society who became romantically involved with an infected woman. It was considered so "risque" it had to be called "DAMAGED GOODS." And not until the medical profession became involved, was it shown as a motion picture in the United States. It brought about an increased interest in the disease and ways of coping with it.

***

There have, however, been mild concessions. An abortion is now allowed in many places when it is clear that the mother's life is in danger. It is allowed also by judges in instances where rape is involved, or if it can be demonstrated that a baby will be born defective. Hospitals, however, are the final arbiters, some refusing to have abortions under any circumstances, and others allowing them only in cases of rape. In many hospitals nuns are on hand during surgery, for whatever reason, to make certain reproductive organs are not tampered with.

***

The prospects for a resolution of the abortion problem in the remaining decades of the 20th century are not very promising. For even many of those who oppose anti-abortion laws and regulations that are sponsored and supported by the Catholic hierarchy and fundamentalist believers in the Old Testament often have an uneasy feeling that the future of a possible human life may be involved in an abortion.

If you want to know what Sigmund Freud thinks about the matter, it is that we can't tell if a newborn infant experiences birth pains the way the mother does, because only a newborn infant can tell us that, and no newborn infant has ever written a book about the way it felt before, during, and after it left the mother's womb to live in a strange, hostile world where everything necessary for survival was no longer automatically provided by the mother.

Finally, let us not forget that even if Congress decided that the most draconic laws will never end abortions and legalized the practice, the sleazy abortionists would not vanish from the scene the way the bootleggers did when liquor was legalized. Thousands of women, without money to pay for abortions by high-priced doctors in meticulously sanitized hospitals will continue to seek out the shady abortionist, or go on risking their lives to create self-induced miscarriages.

Thus, while pledging allegiance to our flag, we will be able to say "with liberty and justice for all" who have money. For what "justice for all," to paraphrase the French author, poet and playwright, Anatole France, means is that whether one is a starving pauper or a millionaire, if one steals a loaf of bread, the penalty for stealing is the same.

SEX AND THE AGE GAP

"It's For All of Us"

I have decided to go for broke, tackle a subject that may shake the world, jolt civilization in a new direction, and cause my younger women friends to label me "a dirty old man" and never again darken the doorstep of my modest home. I am going to debunk the prevailing worldwide belief that there comes a time in their lives when old people lose interest in sex, somewhat the way teenagers lose their interest in dolls and toys, which were once such an important part of their lives. The silence of old people themselves helps perpetuate the myth that for them sex is only a memory along with their first tricycle and first day in school.

It is this picture the world has of old people which enables Bob Hope or George Burns to make audiences laugh uproariously when they say, "I still chase girls, but I don't know why," or allows Milton Berle, in a BVD men's shorts commercial to say, "At my age, I do everything in my BVDs." (Great stuff, Milty. Fall off a chair and break a leg and everybody will laugh even louder.)

***

Mine is not the sort of study students work on for months as they prepare a thesis for a Ph.D. It is based on a conclusion that the sex everyone is talking about and writing about—everyone, that is, except Sigmund Freud—is "genital sex"; the sex that comes with puberty, which begins at eleven and thirteen and continues until sixteen or seventeen, when boys and girls become adults. (I remember a story about a school girl given an assignment on girls growing up, who wrote: "Some girls do not seem to know much about life until they reach the age of adultery.")

Sex is an earlybird. The "bundle from heaven" the happy parents receive contains, among other things, a batch of genes, which become troublesome problems when the loving parents begin their crusade to keep the infant from, as the popular song puts it, "doin' what comes natur'ly." As they house-break a puppy and teach it to heel and roll over, they plunk the infant on a potty and order him or her to "do something," whether they need to eliminate or not. The parents smile when the infant does "something" and are cross when it doesn't. Here begins the art of deception. The infant learns how to please parents and how to irritate them to get what it wants.

Similarly, the infant is not fed when it begins to feel the stomach spasms called epigastralgia. Training begins early to accustom him or her to eat at regular hours that square with the parents' lifestyle. The mother begins to see signs of her male God-sent angel's future sexual activity while bathing him. Before he reaches five, her angel has discovered the pleasant feeling that comes with stroking, what Jewish people call, "der petzele." The mother screams: "If I catch you doing that again, I will cut off that dirty thing with a big knife," without realizing she may have created a future homosexual.

What I am trying to say is that sex is there before the "genital sex" period and after the "genital period," and the myth that old people lose interest in sex at any time in their lives is just that—a myth, funny stories by comedians notwithstanding.

***

When I was nineteen, an aunt of mine married at the age of thirty-six.

I was so disgusted that a women as old as that was still enjoying sex that I became impotent for a whole week. Then, at the age of forty-six, when I was in bed with a woman my age, I lost the ability to perform the sex act when she informed me that she was having a regular sexual relationship with a sixty-two year old owner of a department store. Today, at the age of ninety, I look back at my early seventies and recall Tennyson's lovely line:

"So fresh, so sad, the days that are no more."

It is true that when a man loses the ability to expel semen and a woman "dries up," nobody celebrates the occasion the way they do their golden wedding anniversary. But the world, believe me, doesn't come to an end.

You still get a warm, erotic feeling sitting opposite a pretty lady or a handsome man. Sex is forever, "Vive la sex." Those men and women who tell you that sex becomes nothing but a three-letter word are, as a fellow-journalist once said, either liars or cowards.

MY SIX WIVES

And Other Friendly Women

EVERYONE WHO KNEW ME in Los Angeles was greatly amused upon learning that I had six former wives. They entertained themselves with such brilliant observations as, "You can throw a stick in any direction and probably hit one of Greene's former wives," or "Hey, Bill, why don't you try to make it seven. Seven is lucky shooting craps, maybe you'll pick up a rich widow."

Even though I frequently joined in the clowning, I have always considered my marriages and involvements with other women a disaster, the most distressing guilt-ridden part of my life.

***

Lecturing at Clark College in Worcester, Massachusetts, in 1911, Freud warned his student-listeners not to get involved in debates over what contributes most to the development of a personality—heredity or the environment. "You might as well be arguing whether the carburetor or the petrol contributes most to the operation of an automobile," said the father of psychiatry.

In my case it could not have been anything other than the environment.

Let me take you back to the first decade of this century in czarist Russia and a traumatic event that involved me and two beautiful Russian ladies.

How well I remember that period of my life! The year was 1903 or maybe 1904. I remember it because that was the year everyone in Russia was celebrating the birth of the czar's and czarina's first and only son—little Alexei. That and the traumatic event made such an impression on me, I even remember the Russian anthem everyone was required to sing again and again: "Bo-zhe' cza'rah' khran-yih' sil-ney' dyerzha'vei..." How do you like that! I can't remember the names of all my former wives, but more than three-quarters of a century after the czar's son was born, I remember the words of the Russian national anthem which hailed his arrival. Poor little Alexei proved to be a hemophiliac, and as everyone now knows, was murdered by the communists along with all the other members of the czar's family.

***

Not far from the straggling group of homes that marked the western end of the Jewish ghetto where I was born were a dozen or more huge, deep pits created by peat miners. (This area in the Ukrainian part of Russia remains an important source of peat for the Soviet Union.) The pits were an ugly addition to a scene already made desolate by the nearby shapeless, paint- peeling, haphazardly-placed Jewish homes. But to me and my friend Zelik and the rest of the ghetto children, the pits were a wonderland—a place to meet and play and argue about whose father was the smartest. On mornings when it was not snowing or raining, there was always a mist over the pits, which, for some mysterious reason, always hung the same height above them—exactly three feet. But it was no mystery to my friend Zelik. He said it was God's way of making sure nobody would fall into the pits. At the bottom of the pits, in the summertime, we picked long, narrow leaves, which had a sharp taste and were used by our mothers to make "schav borshch." (When we moved to Canada I found "schav borshch" made with spinach in the stores. My mother said it looked like "pishacts" (urine). She wouldn't touch it and upbraided me for bringing home food that wasn't "kosher.")

On the other side of the pits were apple orchards. In the spring when the wind was in the right direction, we enjoyed taking deep breaths of the wonderful smell from the fragrant blossoms; and in the fall, the branches would become so heavy with apples, the smallest of us could reach them and pick all he wanted.

One afternoon, as I was nearing the pits without Zelik by my side, I saw ahead of me about six or seven of my playmates, strung out in a line with their backs to me, apparently greatly interested in what they were watching. And when I myself was near enough to see what it was, I was so surprised I almost stopped breathing. Two beautiful Russian ladies—I was sure they were beautiful, even though I only saw their backs—were sitting on canvas chairs with easels before them painting the ugly pits against a background of lovely orchards. On their heads were straw hats with large floppy brims, and each wore a white fluffy dress with silk ribbons at the ends of the sleeves, which reached only to their elbows, as well as the necks of their blouses and at the bottom edge of their skirts.

I had never seen anyone like them among the Russian ladies I saw at Easter time in the city outside the ghetto, and certainly not among the Jewish women, young or old, inside the ghetto. After a while, as we all stood there gaping, the two Russian ladies turned their heads to look at the ragged little Jews admiring them. They laughed and returned to their paints and brushes. I was right about them being beautiful. When I saw their lovely delicate faces, I fell in love with them, wildly, passionately, unreasonably. I a ragged little Jew, scratching my itching scalp with the fingers of my right hand, in love with two gentile women. (They were called "barishnyas," the feminine gender of the Russian word "barin"— a nobleman.

When I became a musician and was playing on the Pacific luxury liner SS President McKinley in the twenties, I talked with several of the "barishnyas" who had managed to escape from Lenin's Russia and were working as dancehall girls in the International Settlement of Shanghai.)

Well, I kept my place after the others left to play elsewhere. The two Russian ladies seemed to pay no attention to me. They returned again the next day and the next, missing only one day in the two weeks they spent on their paintings. And I was always there to watch them. I dreamed of them each night, and hardly slept when they failed to turn up. In my dreams, they often turned around and smiled at me. And one time they beckoned, and when I came close they dipped into the chocolate box that was always on the ground between their chairs, and loaded my arms with enough chocolates to take home to my little brother and sister.

One day it really happened. They did turn their heads and looked at me. It was not a dream, and I felt a delicious glow all over me. First one turned

and said something which I could not hear. Then
the other turned her head. But I saw that they were
not smiling. Then the first one screamed at me: "Von
vshivey zhid" and the other, "von bolynoy zhid."

I was stunned, paralyzed; they called me a louse-
ridden Jew, a sick Jew, and they wanted me to get
away from there. I stood staring at my two beautiful Russian ladies, mouth wide open and the tips of
the fingers of my right hand frozen to the scalp I
had been scratching. Then I began sobbing and fled.
It was a dreadful, traumatic experience. I was overwhelmed with shame and said nothing at home, and
mother and grandmother began wringing their hands
in agony because I was withdrawn and ate no more
than a bird; and even that only to please them and
to stop them hovering over me as though I was on
my deathbed.

All of the talk I had heard from my older brother
about the vastness of space and the stars, and my
mother's constant reminder that we Jews were fa-
vorites of God, became mixed up in my mind. I didn't,
of course, want God to go so far as to strike the two
Russian ladies dead for what they had done to one
of his favorite little boys. But in His infinite pity
and understanding, he had saved poor little Isaac
just as Abraham was going to plunge a knife into
his breast. So why couldn't He, at least, have done
something to their voices so that they wouldn't have
been able to call me a louse-ridden, sick little Jew?
It would have taken such little effort from Him to
have done that.

In my new set of dreams I was now full grown
and rich and I was back in Russia from America,
and the two "barishnyas" were in my dreams beg-

ging me to come and sit beside them and eat all the chocolates I was able to eat.

"I need you like I need cholera," I said to them, trying to sound like my father rejecting an offer from a neighbor. "I have a lot of beautiful women in America who love me and all of them are gentiles like you."

***

It was a long time before the memory of the two beautiful Russian ladies completely vanished from my mind and I found myself in bed with a member of the opposite sex. They were always in the back of my mind during my years as a jazz musician, when young women were practically throwing themselves at me and other members of the band. Sex itself did not seem important to me. What seemed important was that the girls were gentiles and I was able to brag about them to the guys. (The memory of the "barishnyas" surfaced again during the forties in Los Angeles when the word "restricted" appeared in the real estate newspaper ads. It was a euphemism for "no Jews.")

Those early jazz-playing days were an almost bizarre period of my life.

I never heard of Freud and knew only that Czar Nicholas was no longer the czar of Russia. Worse still, I did not even realize what my involvement with gentile girls and women might do to my orthodox Jewish parents if they learned about it, which my mother did from the mothers of two other members of the band. When we finally disbanded in 1921, I returned to my home in Winnipeg after an absence of more than three years. I sat the small satchel with all my worldly possessions and my slide trombone on the porch and rang the doorbell. When my mother opened the door, she looked at me, and as if she were talking to somebody else, said: "Look at him, look how thin he is. Where has he been that they didn't give him enough to eat?"

Then, while she stuffed food in me, she started hinting. "Fanny is a such a nice Jewish girl. She always asks about you. I hear she had a quarrel with Aaron Golden." Then, "You remember David Zimster, don't you?

He and Jessie are going to have their first baby in August." Not a word about the rumors; only the hints. To placate my mother, I began going around and bringing home a pretty Jewish girl named Ada Adler. We used to "neck" a lot and arouse each other. But she was so innocent, probably even a virgin, so we didn't go any further. I do not know how it came about, but Ada's mother began spreading the word that Ada and I were going to get married and even sent out the invitations for a reception. That's when I took off for the United States.

***

I cannot help but believe that my childhood in Russia created in me a subconscious feeling of inadequacy and inferiority, and that my struggle for self-improvement and interest in gentile women is related to my dreams about the two beautiful Russian ladies who had humiliated me.

Of my six wives and other women with whom I was intimately involved, only two were Jewish. Both had IQs much higher than mine, and I learned more about the philosophers from them than I did about sex. I remember both of them for their wit and humor. The one who was a World War Two WAC, and was compelled to spend most of her time on a lonely remote Pacific island, made this cogent observation: "It is amazing how many months you can be without sex, and catch up in a few minutes." The other came out of the shower into the kitchen one morning, and I said: "You know, Pearl, without your glasses you look beautiful." And she said: "Without my glasses, you also look beautiful." About one thing, however, I am absolutely certain—I was deeply and passionately involved with only one woman. And with her I fell in love more than a year after I grudgingly married her.

When I talk about my love for her, it is the love Eric Fromm discusses in his book, The Art of Loving. "True love," says Fromm, "is when a woman and a man feel that they are one, in every sense of the word's meaning, and yet both retain their integrity as individuals." And that is the way I felt about beautiful, sensitive Carol. When my arms were around her, I sometimes felt like I would like to crawl inside of her and become a part of her.

***

Carol, who became my second wife, was eighteen years old, slender, wistful, slightly neurotic and a friend of my first wife Irene, with whom I lived for ten years. My life with Irene taught me something all men should know. I mean all those men who think a wife should be content and happy if you do nothing but work and sweat to provide her with a

roof over her head and food for her physical survival. I found out the hard way that isn't enough.

I met Irene while my band was playing for dances
at Glacier Park in Montana. I had by that time developed a great yearning for a home and a wife and
children, and as always happens when you want something
very badly, I saw qualities in her which did not really exist and vice versa.

Her parents were Polish Catholics. She loved dancing,
wrestling, prize fighting and similar cultural activities. When her mother learned more than a week
later that we were married, this is what she said:
"Not only is that son-of-a-bitch not a Catholic, he
isn't even a Christian." I disappointed poor Irene. I
immediately began limiting my musical talent to Saturday
night dances and working as a railroad laborer. We
moved to Washington state, where I worked first as
a laborer, then as a newspaperman, and played for
dances whenever there was spare time.

Nine years passed and I had my first home, but
nothing else. I was a stranger to Irene and our two
children, whom she frequently dragged along with
her to wrestling matches and prize fights. It was, I
have to admit, my fault, not hers. Irene was young.
I made no effort to get her interested in what I was
doing. She might have learned to like it—going to
court and sitting with me near the prosecutor, where
everyone would see her. She might even have learned
how to write up wrestling matches for the paper.

She would have loved it, I am sure.

***

Carol, with an insatiable appetite for knowledge,
fell in love with me because I could talk to her about

Shakespeare, Shelley, and the ballet.

Irene and I were still married. Carol's interest and excitement gave me great pleasure when her face and eyes made clear she understood my step-by-step explanation of how Rene Descartes established the existence of God.

Irene didn't seem to mind. Indeed, one cold night the three of us found ourselves some forty miles from home and decided to stay overnight at a hotel. Carol complained she was cold in her bed and Irene invited her to join us. That, my friends, was a mistake. (I learned years later, that Irene had by that time become interested in a tavern owner in Montana.)

***

One day, while Irene and the children were visiting in Montana, an opportunity presented itself for me to move to Idaho. I saw in this a chance to unravel myself from my growing involvement with Carol. I had begun to see in her signs of mental instability—a beautiful, sex-driven young woman, rebelling against parental prohibition, in search of security an older man might be able to provide. I was torn between a desire to help her, and the conviction that the kind of security I might be able to provide would not help her. She needed a younger, intelligent, understanding man.

I was in Idaho no more than a month when she turned up and moved into my apartment. She was quiet, gentle, pathetic, and irresistible. I felt like I was whipping a whining little puppy when I held her hand and said, "Darling, it would be a mistake to get married. My own life is all screwed up, I got my divorce papers from Irene, but haven't the remotest idea where I'll be a year from now." She listened silently, and said: "I'll go on loving you the rest of my life."

Twice I awakened during the night to find her missing and blood in a pan by the bed. She had slashed her wrists with a razor blade. I found her wandering blindly several blocks from the apartment house both times. My life was a nightmare. During "normal" times, there were days when she became a nymphomaniac, which left me feeling it was I who was developing mental instability. I began to fear for her life and decided to marry her. We drove to neighboring Garfield County in Washington state and were married secretly in a town named Pomeroy. Carol Mehl, born in Mitchell County, Kansas, in 1919, became Mrs. Greene.

***

I had a cunning plan. I would find a handsome man who, I was sure, would be happy to take her off my hands. Everyone would then live happily ever after. Who could possibly resist a beautiful woman whose bosom and face screamed the word "sex." I got her a job as a cigarette girl in the swankiest hotel I could find. But she rejected all offers and advances with a smile, and to persistent come-ons said: "I am Mrs. Greene, you know."

Then the roof caved in. Despite all my careful precautions, she managed to become pregnant, not by accident but deliberately. It was the worst thing that could have happened. I was absolutely flabbergasted. I was tied to her for years. Month eight of her pregnancy was the worst of my life. It was hot in Lewiston, Idaho where I was working. One day the thermometer reached 108. There were, of course, no air conditioners in our apartment, only a noisy electric fan. Carol suffered terribly. She was the ugliest pregnant woman in the world, with a violent temper to match. She screamed at me, cursed everyone, including God. My beautiful, gentle Carol was now an ugly monster with a huge stomach. I watched Carol. She was squirming in her chair in an attempt to be more comfortable, wiping the sweat from her face. Suddenly a thought flashed through my mind. She was doing all this for me. She was going through this horrible ordeal because she loved me. It was a kind of love I never knew existed, and it was for me.

I saw a new Carol. She was again slender and wistful and I was suddenly passionately in love with her. The next few years with Carol and the baby boy, who was born by Caesarean surgery, were the best years of my life. We named him Kirby after my first city editor, Kirby Billingsly. I wish I could conclude with: "And we lived happily ever after," but I can't, for this story had a very tragic ending.

***

Today it is possible to keep a person anesthetized for hours on end. But when Kirby was born, the doctor came out of the delivery room about thirty minutes after the surgery began and told me that in order to save the lives of both Carol and the baby it was necessary to rush things, and that she would probably need additional surgery at some future date. Neither he nor the S.O.B. who performed the second operation in a Spokane hospital about three years later said a word about the dreadful, devastating consequences that might possibly follow a second operation in a case such as Carol's.

It involved the removal of part of the uterus, a hysterectomy.

Sensitive, often neurotic Carol, at the age of 23, began to have hot flashes and all the other symptoms of menopause. The change was incredible. She now talked rationally, but lost interest in me. I dared not touch her. She seemed to fear someone would take Kirby away from her, and would not let the baby out of her sight. I asked her what I could do to help her. I would die for her, I told her, if that would help. She looked thoughtfully at me and said: "Bill, nobody has ever been as good to me as you have been. But I don't love you."

I talked with Spokane's police psychiatrist and he suggested we separate. He said he was sure she would recover. Leaving her alone for a year or so may hasten her recovery. If I did not leave her alone, he said, she might wake up some night, find a knife and kill me, the child, and herself. Before sending her off with Kirby by train to live with her parents, I asked her if I could send her money to help support her and the child. "No," she said, "you have already paid a high price for what has happened. It is nobody's fault. I am sure I will be able to manage."

***

I did not see Carol for twelve years. That's the way she wanted it. I was in Oregon on my vacation and decided to surprise her at a place called The Dalles on the Columbia River, where her new husband was working on a dam project. She was surprised, and I think also pleased. Twelve years had passed and Kirby, now sixteen, seemed uncertain about whether he should be interested in me or not. We spent a pleasant afternoon and evening, never mentioning the past. In the morning, before I left in my car, while Carol prepared breakfast for me, I asked her how Kirby got along with Benny (her husband's surname was Benson) and she replied: "Benny has been wonderful to both of us. He has been generous and understanding, and I don't think a cross word has passed between us. What I so miss is the intellectual stimulation you provided. I remember what you said about the nations having become so utterly interdependent that when a disaster hits one nation, everyone feels it, whether they know it or not. Benny doesn't know that."

I was pleased and sad at the same time.

***

The last time I saw Carol was shortly before she died in 1970 in the Virginia Mason Hospital in Seattle. They had sent her there from Wenatchee, which is east of the Cascade Mountains, for x-ray treatment in a last effort to save her. She had a brain tumor. I was by that time working on a newspaper in Tacoma, thirty miles south of Seattle.

She was 52 years old and knew she was dying. She said very little. I chose my words carefully. I told her I was doing research for a biography of Louise Bryant and went on telling her something of what I had learned about Louise. She asked me a few questions about my work on the Tacoma paper.

Then two hospital attendants came into the room and gently moved her onto another bed and began to wheel her to the x-ray room. As she lifted her right arm in a good-bye gesture, I saw thin horizontal lines of rough skin on her wrists. It was where she had slashed them with a razor blade three decades earlier.

That is why I am so sad as I write about the only woman I truly loved.

You see, there always comes a time when there is no longer much of a future ahead of you. So the bittersweet years of the past become more poignant than ever. And if nobody is around to see you cry, you can't help but shed tears.

THE WOMEN'S STRUGGLE

It's Not Over 'Til It's Over

I AM CONVINCED that nature is to blame for man's egotistical belief that he was created to run the world and that woman's role was to take orders, not to give them. It began long, long ago when man first appeared on this globe. In the beginning he reacted reflexively to his nature- created needs, somewhat the way one's leg kicks out when a doctor taps it with a rubber mallet. Many centuries had to pass before he discovered his mental potential for creating totems and gods and taboos and primitive ethics to explain and justify his behavior.

Meanwhile, he learned very slowly and very clumsily that he could stop the periodic, uncomfortable feeling inside him—today we call it "hunger"—by swallowing berries, leaves and bark. In the same slow, clumsy way he discovered he could end another nature-created tension which surfaced when he came in contact with a female. This time he did not need berries, leaves and bark.

What made it possible for males of that long-forgotten prehistoric past to consider themselves rulers of the world was the indisputable fact that while both males and females needed berries and leaves and bark in order to survive, only the males could devote full time to making these available.

Females, you see, found themselves producing and caring for offspring during nearly all of the fertile years of their lives. The conclusion, insofar as males were concerned, was inescapable. Females were created for the same reason berries, leaves and bark were created—to meet two of man's basic needs. In other words, they were pleasure-providers. As such, they were herded into harems by sultans, used by males as gifts to other males, or could be traded for blankets or horses.

As civilization continued its ponderous march into an endless future, creating improvements in the struggle to live, the male-female relationship began to change. The abolition of polygamy in many parts of the world converted what had often been an unpleasant and unwelcome ritual for women into a personal experience often involving affection and love. Women began to find ways to avoid devoting every moment of their fertile years to making and caring for babies. Then came the Industrial Revolution and man's role as a provider of the means of subsistence changed radically.

But what did not change was man's insistence of supremacy. A woman's place was in the home. They were at their best in the bedroom, in the kitchen, and the children's nursery. The idea of women becoming involved in industrial, mercantile, and political matters was absurd, and as preposterous as the demand by factory workers for a voice in determining the conditions under which they worked.

Near the end of the eighteenth century, Mary Wollstoncroft, the mother- in-law of the great English poet, Percy Bysshe Shelley, wrote a book, The Vindication of the Rights of Women, containing everything that had ever been written before (and since) about the rights of women. When the book was published, it was received with sneers, ridicule, and suggestions that the author belonged in a lunatic asylum. (Mary Wollstoncroft's daughter, the wife of Shelly, wrote the horror story "Frankenstein.") Not surprisingly, many women agreed. There were, after all, still places in the world, and there still are today, where women were required to cover their faces and wear loose, ugly, sack-like clothes so as not to arouse men erotically outside the bedroom. Despite the ridicule that was heaped on Mary Wollstoncroft's book, it became the catalyst for the British women's crusade to participate in the nation's political process. What may come as a surprise, however, is that more than a century after the book was published, Britain, which boasted that it was the first and greatest democracy in the world, became the land where women had the toughest struggle to win the right to vote, with the United States not far behind.

In England, for instance, the British Liberal Party called a mass meeting in Manchester in 1905, at which Sir Edward Grey was to outline what the Liberals would do if they were elected. It was at this meeting that Christabel Parkhurst and Annie Kenney had the temerity to get up and ask what Sir Edward and his Party had in mind for the women who had been campaigning for political rights. "Troublemakers, troublemakers...throw them out," screamed everybody. A pair of husky males grabbed them, kicked them down the stairs, and did just that. "We will now go on with the meeting," said Sir Edward.

Outside, Mrs. Parkhurst and Mrs. Kenney tried to address the crowd that had collected. They were arrested for obstructing the sidewalk and fined.

They chose to go to jail. A great many women had, by that time, become involved in the women's struggle, and it became clear to them that they would get nowhere by appealing to the humane side of men or by signing petitions. They adopted the technique of violence. They began smashing windows and destroying private and public property. Sent to prison, they staged hunger strikes. The authorities tried to feed them forcibly, and when this didn't work, they were paroled, but not for very long—only until they were strong enough to be dragged back to prison to serve out their sentences. Emily Davison, a militant protester, threw herself in front of the horses at a Derby race in 1913 and was killed trying to dramatize the crusade.

Every known trick in the parliamentary book, and some that were not in the book, were used to stall proposals to give women the vote. This reached its lowest and meanest point the same year in which Davison died. The prime minister, Herbert Asquith, announced a measure in parliament to reform the voting laws and said he would accept women's suffrage amendments. The amendments came so thick and fast, and some were so ludicrous, that the whole voting reform plan was dropped. It wasn't until 1928 that English women got full voting rights. So much for the proud British boast that "Britons never shall be slaves."

***

In the United States, masculine determination to keep women where they would be most useful never showed up better than immediately after the Civil War, fought to free the Negro slaves. Among the most vigorous and vocal opponents to Negro slavery were Sarah and Angeline Grimke, Lucretia Mott, Elizabeth Stanton, Lucy Stone and Susan Anthony, along with many other women. But when the war had been fought and won, the amendment to the Constitution spoke only of rights for the freed slaves. The women, who had been campaigning for political rights since 1840, found their pleas falling on deaf ears. It would have been little consolation to them had they been clairvoyant enough to know that, even with legislation, nobody would pay much attention to the amendments barring Negro discrimination for another hundred years.

Three suffragette groups were involved in the American struggle for women's political rights. The most militant group was the National Women's Party. Its members had become convinced that only by adopting the tactics of the British suffragettes would men in Congress ever agree to submit to the states an Amendment to the Constitution giving women the right to vote.

They had tried the peaceful way by standing on street corners and distributing handbills, only to be harassed, spat upon, ridiculed, and called vulgar names.

***

On February 14, 1919, the New York Times headlines screamed:

"SUFFRAGETTISTS BURN WILSON IN EFFIGY. MANY LOCKED UP. POLICE STOP DEMONSTRATIONS BEFORE WHITE HOUSE ON EVE OF AMENDMENT VOTE. VIOLENT SPEECHES MADE."

"Police," said the dispatch from Washington, "were reluctant to give a list of all who had been arrested. However, those known to be in durance (a rarely used word for imprisonment, which reporters sometimes threw in to show that they were erudite) from New York include Mrs. H. O. Havemeyer, Miss Cora Weeks, Miss Louise Bryant, Miss Edith Ainge, Miss Amy Gungling, Miss Lucy Burns and Mrs. Chevler. Estimates of the number of women arrested range from forty to sixty-five, and estimates of the size of the demonstration vary, but all agree it was the most impressive the militant National Women's Party had staged so far."

This was only one of the scores of demonstrations that militant women were staging throughout the United States the night before the Senate was to vote again on an amendment to grant women the right to vote. A reading of newspapers for 1919 makes hard-to-believe reading today. Women battled police, broke picket signs over the heads of the guardians of the law, boycotted merchants whose wives didn't join the crusade, went on hunger strikes, and chained themselves to telephone poles to make it difficult for police to haul them off to jail before they had finished their speeches.

The target of the demonstrations on the eve of the Senate's vote on the 19th Amendment (it lost again, this time by one vote) was President Woodrow Wilson. He had finally become converted to the cause of women's political rights, but the militants felt he wasn't doing enough to assure passage of the Amendment. He had, as a matter of fact, sent telegrams to key senators urging approval, but women said it was too little and too late. He was the head of the Democratic Party, and they wanted him to put pressure, real pressure, on southern senators who had nightmares in which long lines of Negro women were voting against them. They had managed to keep Negro men from voting despite the 14th and 15th Amendments, but these crazy militant women—who could tell what they might not do?

"The effigy of President Wilson, which looked like a huge doll stuffed with straw and was slightly over two feet in height," said the New York Times, "was dropped into the flames by Miss Sue White...there was a good deal of confusion as the district police, the military police, and the Boy Scouts, who assisted in the roundup of the women, were getting busy. Miss White made the following statement before she was pushed into the police patrol wagon: 'We burn not the effigy of the President of a free people, but the leader of an autocratic party organization whose tyrannical power holds millions of women in political slavery...Mr. Wilson, as the leader of his party, has forgotten, or else he never knew, the spirit of true democracy...We feel that this protest will shock Mr. Wilson and his followers and put into action the principle that those who submit to authority shall have a voice in their government.'" And Mrs. Havemeyer of New York fought off those who were dragging her to the patrol wagon long enough to yell: "Every government in the world has enfranchised its women.

In Russia, in Hungary, in Austria—in Germany thirty-four women are not sitting in the new Reichstag. We women of America are here today to voice our deep indignation that while America is devoting its energies to establishing democracy in Europe, American women remain deprived of a voice in their government."

EXTRA! EXTRA! Read All About It... NEW YORK— Carrying banners on which were inscribed, "Mr. President, How Long Must Women Wait for Suffrage?" "An Autocrat at Home is a Poor Champion of Democracy Abroad." Two hundred militant suffragettes attempted to stage a demonstration at Broadway and Fortieth Street against President Wilson. For more than two hours a cordon of police had its hands full trying to keep them from crashing through the lines. Time after time they attached the patrolmen and civilians with their banners and fingernails only to be repulsed by the police. WASHINGTON—While the Senate debated the Suffrage Amendment before defeating it, the galleries were packed with women, which gave the Senate chamber the appearance of a style show. The women wore the latest and showiest apparel and the most colorful millinery. The ushers were careful to separate the militants, who burned President Wilson in effigy, from the less belligerent suffragists. The anti-suffragists were allotted a gallery by themselves. Senator Wadsworth of New York, whose wife is a member of the suffragists, voted against the Amendment. PHILADELPHIA—Miss Louise Bryant, wife of well known Bolshevist propagandist, John Reed, was arrested here yesterday and charged with resisting arrest and disorderly conduct after she refused police orders to end a street corner lecture on the subject of women's suffrage. The disorderly conduct charge was added when she allegedly addressed the police in unprintable language. WASHINGTON—Police put an end to a foot race in Lafayette Square tonight between angry crowds of men and three torch bearing sentinels of the militant National Women's Party by arresting the women. They refused to furnish bail. A statement by the party's headquarters said: "Our liberty fires are a symbol of our contempt for words unsupported by deeds. We will not sit in silence while the President presents himself to the people of Europe as the representative of a free people, when the American women are not free, and he is chiefly responsible for it." WASHINGTON—Senator Jones of New Mexico today announced plans to introduce a resolution which would confer the right of franchise upon women, but only to a number in each state that does not exceed the number of men voting.

(The 19th Amendment to the United States Con-

stitution, giving women the right to vote, was finally passed by the House on May 21, 1919, and the
Senate on June 4, 1919. It then went to the states for
ratification.) WASHINGTON—There is every indi-
cation that from now on the warfare between women
suffragists and anti-suffragists over ratification of
the Federal Suffrage Amendment will be carried on
with more regressiveness by both sides. With adop-
tion of the Amendment by Congress the battleground
has shifted to the states. Both sides have moved their
headquarters from here to New York. WASHING-
TON—The militant suffragettes represented by the
National Women's Party tonight announced plans
for a "Prison Special" train to tour the country and
whip up support in the states for ratification of the
Federal Suffrage Amendment. The women who will
make up the contingent aboard what they call the
"Democracy Limited" are those who have served jail
terms for picketing. They intended to wear costumes
resembling those they wore in jail, but rail authorities rejected their demand to have the train painted
to resemble a prison. ATLANTA—The Federal Suffrage Amendment was defeated in both houses of
the Georgia General Assembly today. Not only was
the bill defeated in both houses, but a move to have
the matter submitted to a vote by the people at the
next white primary was voted down. Senator Rigsdale
declared that if the bill passed, "It would mean that
the American race would be degraded and wiped
off the face of the earth."

***

Three score and eight years after the 19th Amendment
became a part of the Supreme Law of the land, it is

well to make an inventory of what it has achieved for the women who had fought so hard for it. The Amendment itself is a simple two-sentence statement to the effect that the right of people to vote should not be denied to them on account of sex. It does not say why it was necessary to have such an amendment, as the Constitution does in the Second Amendment about guns: "A well-regulated militia being necessary to the security of a free state, the right of the people to keep and bear arms shall not be infringed."

Consider the controversy that has developed over the one-sentence Second Amendment. By eliminating the part that tells us why the amendment was needed, the gun shooters have managed to bamboozle the nation into believing that every American has a constitutional right to own and carry a gun even though the courts have ruled again and again that it relates to the militia. In any event, the constitutional right to vote does not solve problems. It merely provides the means for solving them. So today, the struggle is over the Equal Rights Amendment and economic rights. I suggest that three score and eight years from now, if the world remains intact, the struggle for ERA will appear as preposterous as the struggle for the right to vote does today. The American philosopher, George Santayana, was right:

"Those who forget history are doomed to relive it."

In today's struggle there seem to remain vestigial elements in the male-female relationship. Remember when women were considered commodities and their male owners could do as they like with them? Then, when polygamy ended, men had to be bribed with dowries to accept them as their wives?

Today all of that is gone. But don't forget it's still the bride's parents who pick up the tab for the wedding. The least the in-laws could do is make it Dutch treat.

THE YEARS OF TRAINS AND DAMS

The Grand Coulee Dam Miracle

IN MY MIDDLE TWENTIES I was still "rolling with the punch." I had no goal for the future, except for a vague desire to be rich without having to work. I adjusted my needs to my environment, and that kept changing. I had been a factory and farm laborer, a welder's assistant, and a baggage smasher hauling heavy wagons of mail bags and luggage on passenger train platforms.

In some places, I also supplemented my income with the help of my slide trombone by playing for Saturday night dances with local orchestras. When we heard the sounds of jazz, which originated in New Orleans, I shifted gears. With a trumpet player friend, I formed a five-piece jazz band and toured Canada. In the United States, I alternated between playing with jazz bands and being a drifter, often traveling in railroad freight cars with members of the radical Industrial Workers of the World, usually called the Wobblies.

During all those years, it never once occurred to me that what destiny had in store for me was a career as a newspaperman, that I would be writing stories to help promote a small town publisher's "crazy" idea for building a giant dam on a river in a rattlesnake-infested desert, and that his "pipe dream" would become a reality. It seems even odder now that I might not have become a journalist involved in the project if I wasn't Jewish.

n 1928 I was living in Wenatchee (pop. about 11,000) in the central part of Washington state. It boasted of being the Apple Capital of the nation. It was also

a division point on the Great Northern Railway between Spokane and Seattle. Division points were places
where locomotives and their crews were changed.
Arriving locomotives were checked and double- checked
and necessary repairs were made by machinists,
boilermakers, electricians and others before the locomotive could again be put into service. I had become a machinist's helper in Wenatchee's Great Northern
Railway roundhouse. You see, I had become convinced that a jazz musician's life was a dead-end
for me. I had, for one thing, realized that I would
never be a top-notch musician and that "Hold That
Tiger" and "12th Street Rag" was not what life was
all about.

***

Of everything involved in building America, nothing
remains as close to so many American hearts as does
the railroad era. Producing replicas of everything
from tiny toy locomotives to forty thousand dollar
railroad facilities that cover a large room for wealthy
folks keeps an entire industry busy. When I began
contributing my share to what is today an important part of Americana, railroading was a romantic
enterprise, especially for those who were involved
in running the passenger trains. How grand the crews
looked to the people chained to the small and large
towns that dotted the vast, lonely prairies of the United
States and Canada. It was the crews of the railroads
that brought and carried away the mail, guests and
newlyweds. Station platforms, believe me, always
hummed with talk, greetings and goodbyes.

In those days, I must remind you, the unions in

railway roundhouses, such as the ones in which I worked, were busted with the help, unfortunately, of the unions of engineers, firemen, conductors and brakemen—so that wages were low, hours long, and working conditions deplorable.

But even my backbreaking work as a laborer was mitigated by discovery after discovery of the intriguing way machinists, boilermakers and others improvised ways to handle mechanical problems involved in servicing and repairing locomotives to assure their safety.

For instance, a hostler and his helper maneuvered a locomotive into the roundhouse. One of its huge steel tires had developed flat spots when the engineer was forced to slam on the brakes. There were no jacks to put under an axle to lift the locomotive slightly off the track. You studied the weight of the engine and the damaged wheel's relation to the other wheels.

Then you got some large steel wedges to put under the other wheels—not under all of them—only those which would affect the one you were trying to lift. The hostler and his helper had been standing by. The hostler got into the locomotive cab. He took hold of the throttle. The machinist nodded to the helper. The helper, keeping his eyes on the machinist, extended both arms and moved them slowly, very slowly, up and down as a signal to the hostler. The locomotive wheel rose about the tracks, and a quick horizontal slash by the machinist stopped the locomotive. Even the task of removing the damaged steel tire from its wheel was not available in a "how-to" guide. The machinist had it heated with welder's torches until it expanded sufficiently to have it removed and hauled to a machine where it was whirled rapidly and the surface shaved and smoothed.

Everything was exciting for me. I wondered how leaking rivets inside the locomotives were located and repaired, how cold locomotive steam was generated inside the roundhouse, and how locomotive wheel brakes worked.

Under each car of a long train was a cylinder containing a plunger with a rod that stuck out. At the end of the rod was a brake that rested on the wheel. A pump in the locomotive fed air to both sides of the plunger inside the cylinder. When the engineer pushed a handle slightly forward, the air pressure was immediately reduced in all of the cylinders on the side where the rods were located. The unaffected air pressure from the other side pushed the plungers forward and the rods and brakes against the wheel.

But I think my most interesting job before I became a machinist's helper was that of a hostler's helper, especially when the hostler happened to be Ray Lawrence. When an engineer brought a locomotive to the roundhouse, Ray and I got busy. Ray would get into the cab and spot the locomotive under the huge water spout, and it was my job to fill the tank with water. Then I also filled the fuel tank with oil. The combination water and fuel oil car attached behind the locomotive was called a "tender" and was always referred to as "she" and not "it." This, according to Ray and other railroad men, was because a "she's" behind was more "tender" than a "he's." You would have to believe this if you knew that an engineer was a "hoghead," a fireman a "tallowpot," seniority "whiskers," a switching engine a "goat," and if you drew your thumb quickly over the fly of your pants, it was a signal for "goat's" engineer to haul the car to the "rip track" for repair.

When we were finished in the roundhouse, we backed the locomotive toward the turntable. The roundhouse itself was a large, brick, half- circular structure, with only the outside half-circle walled in. Two dozen sets of rails began inside the building and extended outside like the spokes of a wheel, ending at the end of a huge round concrete pit. In the center of this pit was a heavy steel column supporting a narrow bridge with a pair of tracks in its center. The column with its bridge was so precisely balanced it could easily be turned and the tracks lined up with any pair of those which led into the roundhouse. When we reached the turntable, the tracks on the bridge were already lined up with the locomotive's tracks, and I jumped from the cab and the locomotive began to back onto the bridge very slowly. Ray watched my hands, and when the huge locomotive reached the exact center and the entire bridge began to rock gently like a child's teeter-totter, I stopped him. I threw a switch and a small motor under the bridge began to move the ponderous load until we reached the tracks of an empty roundhouse stall. Then came two toots and the entire mass lumbered into the roundhouse.

One day I decided to eat my lunch in the cab of a locomotive that had not yet been serviced. I sat down on the engineer's side of the cab. I had never touched the throttle in the cab of a locomotive. When I finished my lunch, I suddenly felt an urge to see what it felt like to move one. I neutralized the brakes, pushed the direction lever, and reached for the throttle. I pulled it forward slightly and the huge mass of steel seemed to hurtle forward. I screamed for help, and several Japanese laborers began to laugh as I slammed on the brakes.

I actually moved only six or seven feet. But the feeling of power, the ability to move a massive locomotive at the touch of a throttle stayed with me for years.

***

The arrival of my second child forced me to take a better-paying job as a machinist's helper. I continued to play for dances on Saturday nights and devoted every spare moment to self-education. What helped me greatly were the little Haldeman-Julius blue books that helped so many others. You could get twenty of them by sending one dollar to Girard, Kansas, where they were published. They were abridged versions of the work of the world's greatest writers on every imaginable important subject.

Everything changed for me one day when I was helping a powerfully built, handsome machinist named Florian Bauer. He had noticed that in spare moments I often pulled from the back pocket of my overalls one of my little blue books. One day he asked me what it was. It happened to be Tom Paine's Age of Reason, an attack on organized religion. He looked surprised.

The events that led me to what is known today as the communications media, are those, I think you will agree, of a low-budget movie in which things happen that hardly ever do in real life. Consider the following chronology: Florian Bauer, the handsome machinist, showed interest in what I was reading, and we became close friends on and away from our jobs. He told his wife Arlene about my interest in an education. Arlene, a ravishing redhead, was the society editor of Wenatchee's newspaper, the Daily World.

I owned an old rattletrap Ford and began stopping at their home to pick up Florian on my way to work. While Arlene made sandwiches for Florian's lunch, she pressed me for information about my background—my Jewish parents, my life in Russia, anti-Semitism and so on. On one such occasion, she asked me if I would like to work on a newspaper. She had talked to Kirby Billingsley, the city editor, about me and he expressed an interest in meeting me. All I knew about newspapers was what I had learned in my early teenage years—how to fold them so that they would land on porches as I passed by on my bicycle. And all the writing I ever did was a few letters and an advertisement or two to put in the newspapers during my jazz band days. But I said, "Yes." Kirby Billingsley (he remains a close friend and one of my sons is named after him) was one of those Christians who took very seriously the words of the Sermon on the Mount. He also believed that the Jews were God's Chosen People and that helping one of His People would certainly please God. I was hired. Add to all this Rufus Woods, the owner-publisher of the Daily World, who vanished one day and surfaced as a clarinet-playing clown in a circus, and you have, as I said, all the elements you need for a low-budget movie.

Rufus Woods was anything but a clown. A stocky, 50 year old man with bushy eyebrows and penetrating eyes, he had only one objective—the development of central Washington state. To this he devoted everything he had—time, money, the newspaper...everything. Traveling through the area (I frequently accompanied him) he would stop off unexpectedly in apple orchards, on wheat farms, in banks, in pool halls, in stores... "I am Rufus Woods of the Daily World...what do you need around here?...do you have an interesting story?...you need a library?...we'll get one for you, be sure to drop in to say hello if you're in Wenatchee." That was Rufus Woods' style.

He told us to avoid using, if possible, the word "Wenatchee" in stories. He wanted everyone everywhere to feel that the Daily World was THEIR newspaper.

It didn't take long in this job before his view of what one needs to be a good newspaperman sunk in. I was alone in the newsroom one evening when the manager of the Cascadian Hotel called by phone and said the president of the Pennsylvania Railroad, William W. Atterbury, was dining with friends at the hotel. It was a big story, because apple freight rates were an important issue in the fruit industry. I sat paralyzed by the telephone when Rufus came in to write his daily column for tomorrow's paper. When he asked what was wrong with me, I told him about the call.

"I don't know who to write a story like that, Mr. Woods," I said. "I am still just watching the tele-type machine so the paper doesn't bungle up.

I answer the phone and if it's a little story I write it and Kirby corrects it next morning."

Rufus' reply was as unconventional as everything else about him: "You can teach a horse to write but what will he have to say? Atterbury's father sent him to Harvard or Yale and for all I know bought him the Pennsylvania Railroad. You're doing it all by yourself. A short time ago you were working in a railway roundhouse and here you are in a profession without which democracy would die. It's what you have to say that counts and not the way you say it, and you have a lot to say that's important."

The next day I talked with Mr. Atterbury in his personal car on his special train. I asked him if he went to Yale or Harvard and he said, "Yale 1866." I don't remember what else he said, but I have never forgotten what Rufus said: "You can teach a horse to write but what will he have to say."

As I began to gain confidence and Kirby Billingsley decided to assign me to cover police, the sheriff's office and city and county officials, Rufus had some more advice for me. "Don't get yourself liked too well by the public officials. When you question them, imagine you're a reader who wants to know something. When I start getting letters telling me what a cooperative reporter you are, I'll tell Kirby to fire you. When I want somebody who reports only what they have to say, I'll hire somebody who knows shorthand."

Long before I joined the staff of the Daily World, Rufus became deeply involved in a "ridiculous" project that had become an obsession for him. It was a project that involved harnessing the Columbia River—a mighty river which had the greatest potential for hydroelectric development in all of North America.

***

The Columbia River originates in British Columbia in Canada and weaves 1,210 miles from its source, across the border and through Washington state to the Pacific Ocean. The lower part becomes the border of Oregon and Washington. That was not always the course of the river. During the ice age, millions of years ago, a glacier began grinding its way slowly southward and at a point in central Washington, 225 miles east of Seattle, blocked and forced the river into a new channel. Then, millions of years later, a geological cataclysm—perhaps the one that caused the Pacific Ocean to crash through the coast line and flood the mountainous valley that is now Puget Sound—enabled the Columbia River to flow to the ocean in its original bed. The abandoned river bed became known as Grand Coulee.

On a blazing hot day in August of 1930 I saw Grand Coulee for the first time when I was with Rufus on one of his periodic trips to Grant County.

You didn't see Grand Coulee in 1930 the way you saw Niagara Falls, Hot Springs or other natural phenomena when you visited them. The Grand Coulee was fifty-two miles long and from one to five miles wide. Nearby Dry Falls, however, was an awesome sight with its mute red and green streaked cliffs, over which once thundered a cataract mightier than Niagara Falls. I was standing beside Rufus on a bluff overlooking the Columbia River. All that we could see in this huge desolate part of Washington state were rolling hills buried in sagebrush, and dust that extended for miles beyond our limited vision.

"One of these days," said Rufus, "this desert will bloom like Eden. All that we need is a big slab of cement across this river."

And a big slab of cement was what the "pipe dream" project was all about. (It was, by the way, an idea that did not originate with Rufus. A Grant County lawyer named Billy Clapp revealed it to him in 1918.)

That big slab of cement would become a dam where the glacier blocked the river millions of years ago. The dam's generators would create electricity for pumps which would raise water from the river and pour it into the Grand Coulee. This would convert the river into a huge water reservoir from which canals would irrigate more than two million acres of what had been dry, useless land for so many centuries. In addition, the dam's generators would produce far more electricity than the pumps would need. This would provide electric power, not only for the newly-created Eden, but also for distant homes and industries. And there is still more. The dam would, of course, hold back the river and the river would become a smooth lake that would go back to the Canadian border and beyond. It would, in other words, become a recreation area for boats, fishing and swimming, and hot dog stands. The prospects and possibilities that would accrue from building a dam at Grand Coulee were incalculable. "All we need is a big slab of cement," said Rufus. It was that easy. It turned out to be as easy as becoming a millionaire. All you need to become a millionaire is a million dollars.

Opposition was overwhelming. The criticisms aimed at the Wright brothers, Alexander Bell, and Thomas Edison were gentle rebukes compared with the ridicule heaped on my poor boss Rufus and his "crazy" proposal.

The most serious attacks came from the private power companies, notably the Washington Power Company in Spokane, about ninety miles east of the proposed dam site. They were all for irrigating central Washington, and submitted elaborate plans for bringing water to the area from eastern Washington and Idaho, but they were vigorously opposed to publicly-

owned utilities and the cheapest power rates in the
nation. A giant dam in central Washington would
be a disaster for them.

General George W. Goethals, who built the Pan-
ama Canal, which also happened to be fifty-two miles
long, signed a report endorsing the private utilities'
plan. Critics scoffed that if a dam were built there
would be no homes and factories to use its power,
and few farms to use its power for irrigation.
Many newspapers and magazines eagerly joined
in the attack.

"Of all the outrages on agriculture...we are beginning to think the Columbia Basin project takes the
cake," the Farm Journal wrote. "Who wants it?

Nobody!"

Well, Rufus wanted it and he wasn't giving up.
He attended sessions of the state legislature to lobby
for the dam. He journeyed to Washington D.C. to
badger senators and congressmen. On one trip to
the capitol he met with A. O. Davis, head of the
U.S. Reclamation Service. "You haven't got a dam
there," Davis told him. Davis was persuaded to come
to Grand Coulee. He tramped two days over the rugged
site and was converted. But the fight was long and
uphill. For thirteen years not a single daily newspaper in the state, except the Daily World, had a good
word for the project.

Little by little, however, the dam idea began to
catch on. First, a few prominent individuals got behind it. Then farm groups and chambers of com-
merce began endorsing it. But critics in Congress
continued to scoff.

"Grand Coulee Dam," Congressman Francis Culkin
said, is the most colossal fraud in the history of America."

When no action was forthcoming from Congress, Rufus went back to Washington to call on President Hoover, whom he revered as "the great engineer." Rufus said the dam should provide power as well as irrigation so that in time it could pay for itself. He reminded Hoover he had once said in a 1926 Seattle speech that "every drop of water that runs to the sea without yielding its full commercial return to the nation is an economic waste." Hoover was sympathetic, but not encouraging. With the country in a depression, he said, he couldn't see where the money to build the dam would come from. "He seemed tired and discouraged," Rufus told us on his return.

***

Chelan County, of which Wenatchee is the county seat, was solidly Republican before Franklin Roosevelt was swept into the White House, and many other Democrats followed him into state and county offices.

Republicans of Chelan County had always looked upon Democrats about the way the ancient Hebrews looked upon the uncouth Philistines when they arrived in Canaan. The exceptions were those Democrats whose grandparents left the South after the Civil War and remained Democrats in name only. But Rufus, I feel certain, would have made a deal with Satan if he believed the Evil One could get the Grand Coulee Dam project moving. So it did not surprise anyone when he got aboard Franklin D. Roosevelt's campaign train when he came through the state and told him about the Grand Coulee Dam. Roosevelt defeated Hoover and began to look for projects to create employment. Then it happened!

I will always remember that Saturday in April of 1933. It was after four in the afternoon and the presses were through with the day's run. A few of us were still in the newsroom. A Western Union messenger boy came in with a telegram for Rufus, and we directed him to the boss's cluttered office. A few moments later Rufus came out wreathed in smiles. He handed us the yellow piece of paper. It was a telegram from Senator C. C. Dill. President Roosevelt, he said, had personally approved $63 million to start work on Grand Coulee Dam. We were so surprised we could not react immediately with the usual "hip, hip hoorays." Rufus was pleased, but far from happy. He knew that a struggle was ahead to get funds for a high dam that was necessary if the Grand Coulee project was to provide the huge amount of contemplated electric energy for pumps and widespread distribution. The private utilities would fight that and congressional reluctance was certain because the New Deal was just getting underway with hundreds of priorities for social programs. Rufus had us all work overtime to get out a special edition explaining the Grand Coulee project, which he sent to every member of Congress. Across it he splashed the headline: TWO MILLION WILD HORSES! That was how much energy, the story explained, the dam would produce.

The battle raged on. Washington state newspapers still opposed the dam. Some called it "creeping socialism," others "visionary" and "impractical." If there was anything that made Rufus mad it was to be called a visionary and a dreamer. He was a self-made businessman and a staunch Republican. But he believed that Grand Coulee would not only be a great plus for the nation, it would also pay for itself. Meanwhile, work on the dam got underway. In 1933 engineers began digging a thirty-five acre hole to bedrock. A conveyor belt, fed by a fleet of trucks, hauled forty-four million tons of earth a mile and a half over a hill and dumped it into Rattlesnake Canyon. Not long afterward, even nature joined in complicating the building of the dam. While engineers dug toward bedrock, a great mass of clay began sliding into the excavation. The engineers stopped it cold—literally. They froze it. Six miles of pipe were driven through the mass of clay. Then salt water, at zero temperature, was circulated through the pipes, freezing the oozing mass until the excavation could be completed.

In 1936, President Roosevelt approved the high dam, and the "big slab of concrete" began to grow taller. Daily, an engineering miracle evolved as nearly nine thousand men, from steeplejacks to deep sea divers, swarmed over the vast dam. The base alone spread over an area nearly three times of that covered by the Great Pyramid of Egypt. President Roosevelt visited the dam to inspect the progress. The dam, he said, in a very correct sense was a "national undertaking."

***

In 1941, twenty-three years after the uphill battle began, the gigantic task of building the dam was completed. There she stood—"Rufus' pipe dream"—the biggest concrete structure on earth. The dam itself rose as high as a forty-six story building, and was more than twelve city blocks across. Behind it lay a lake which extended 151 miles to the Canadian border. The mighty waterfall, hurtling over the dam, was higher than towering Victoria Falls in Africa, and twice as powerful as Niagara Falls.

EPILOGUE:

Rufus died in 1950 at the age of 72 while he was in Canada studying the Ontario power system. His final rites were held in the Wenatchee park where the old town band used to play when he first came to town as a young man. A decade after his death, I decided to make a "sentimental pilgrimage" from Los Angeles, where I was living, to central Washington. What I saw confirmed the Old Testament's Ecclesiastes: "Time and chance happeneth to all."

If I wanted to see what happened to the endless rolling hills once buried in sagebrush and dust, which Rufus predicted would "bloom like Eden," I would have to charter an airplane. I don't think Adam, who is supposed to have been Eden's first tenant, would like New Eden, U.S.A., unless he was reincarnated and became a capitalist entrepreneur.

What I saw myself, what the actual figures of growth and expansion I was shown revealed, might have been unimpressive to visiting tourists, but to those of us who tramped through the hot desert, wearing high boots to protect against rattlesnakes, it was an amazing transformation.

The Grand Coulee Dam's stored waters had created the nation's largest reclamation project. More and more land was being irrigated. The population was rapidly increasing, homes were being built, a sugar plant was busy, as was a Boeing jet testing facility. What was once a wasteland of sand and sagebrush has become a checkerboard of fertile farms producing bumper crops of everything imaginable. Water from the dam turned the desert into a bird sanctuary and a mecca for sportsman and vacationers. Where once there were only alkali flats, there was now a network of sparkling lakes.

It was not a "pipe dream." It was a miracle.

FLIGHT INTO HISTORY

The Epochal Trans-Pacific Venture

I am sure that I would have considered the weekend of October 3-5 in 1931 one of the most exciting of my life, even if it wasn't also an important event in aviation history.

The event: Four years after Charles Lindbergh's 1927 historic flight in a Ryan monoplane from New York to Paris, two American flyers took off from a beach near Tokyo for the world's first trans-Pacific flight to the United States and landed in Wenatchee in central Washington. This is my recollection of the extraordinary way a small town's newspaper staff covered the event and how the news reached the world.

***

ABOUT EIGHT OF US were crowded into the small room that was part of the hangar where Frank Kammer, the owner-pilot, kept his airplane. Outside was the airfield—a stretch of land in the hills above the Columbia River.

There were no runways, only rough grass. On the other side of the Columbia, some five miles distant over rough country road, was Wenatchee.

Three of us were newspaper people, including myself from the Wenatchee paper, and the others were from Seattle and Spokane. There were, of course, photographers. It was early Monday morning, October 5, 1931. Most of us had been there since before midnight Sunday on the small chance that Clyde Pangborn and Hugh Herndon might land there. They had taken off from Japan about a day and a half earlier for the world's first non-stop trans-Pacific flight in a monoplane Belanca, but nobody had heard from them since they had left Sabishiro Beach near Tokyo; no ship had sighted them and nobody knew if they were still somewhere over the Pacific or if they had crashed and perished.

Our hope that they might land in Wenatchee, if they made it, was based on the fact that Clyde Pangborn's brother was a Wenatchee businessman and his mother lived there. But prior to takeoff there was a dispatch from Japan that indicated they would probably try to land somewhere else—somewhere where there were better landing facilities. This, we all knew, they would certainly need. For not only could this desolate stretch of land in the hills near Wenatchee hardly be called an airfield, the Pangborn- Herndon plane would have to come down without landing gear. They had dumped it in the ocean after takeoff on account of the heavy load of gasoline they were forced to carry for the long flight.

Still, we waited hopefully. Kirby Billingsley, at that time city editor of the Daily World, had even made arrangements with the telephone company for operators to clear an immediate line from the airfield to the newspaper office, and another line to the Associated Press in Seattle, just in case they did land. So we waited. But about four in the morning we gave up and began to drift away. There was only one old-fashioned wall telephone anyhow, and Carl Cleveland, who later became an executive with the Boeing Company in Seattle, volunteered to stay on.

I got into my jalopy and bumped my way over

the rutted road to the Daily World office in Wenatchee. Kirby Billingsley was already there. A few minutes later reporter Bob Thomas arrived from the airfield, and other members of the staff began to drift in. Several hours passed. Some of us slept on the mailroom benches. By seven a.m. we were all awake and organizing ourselves for the usual Monday morning newspaper chores.

***

Then it came. We heard it and we saw it. It was a beautiful October morning and the plane appeared in the sky northwest of Wenatchee. It was a stirring, inspiring sight. The plane, minus landing gear, was heading for the airfield in the hills on the east side of the Columbia River. And just at the moment the plane in sight, one of the telephones rang. I dived for it. Kirby Billingsley grabbed another to the Associated Press in Seattle.

"It's hear...it's here," Cleveland was shouting into the wall telephone at the airfield. "It's here...it's here," I yelled at Billingsley. And Billingsley echoed my words into the phone for the Associated Press in Seattle.

In Seattle an AP man was repeating Billingsley's words for operators who punched them out on their keyboards for instant transmission to teletype machines in newspaper offices all over the nation, and cablegrams elsewhere in the world.

It was a fantastic operation. The very first news of this epochal flight to come over the teletypes everywhere in the United States were just the words and phrases shouted by Carl Cleveland into his telephone. They came back on our own teletype machine in the Daily

World office like an echo.

In the airfield office there were a couple of small windows through which Cleveland could see what was going on.

"They're circling," he screamed. "They're just above me...wait...they're dumping gasoline...they're going to land...they have landed...they're traveling on the ground on the belly of the plane."

We were almost beside ourselves with excitement.

At one point Cleveland shouted that something seemed to have happened and the plane was suddenly in a perpendicular position with the propeller end on the ground. Then it began to teeter on the broken prop. Was it going to land on its back or on its belly? It seemed aged before Cleveland shouted that the plane had landed on its belly, and Clyde Pangborn and Hugh Herndon walked out grinning after 41 hours and 13 minutes in the air, during which they had covered 4,600 miles (the Lindbergh flight figures were 3,610 miles and 33-1/2 hours).

***

Wenatchee went wild. Before the day was over the town was full of newspapermen, photographers, and dignitaries from everywhere. As soon as photographs were available Frank Kammer warmed up his small Ryan, and accompanied by reporter Bob Thomas, headed across the Cascades for the Associated Press offices at Portland and San Francisco.

As for Pangborn and Herndon, they appeared to be less excited than anyone else in Wenatchee. Indeed, I got the impression that they were somewhat puzzled by all the excitement and furor being made over them.

Asked which was the most thrilling moment of the entire remarkable flight, Herndon said it came when the fuel from one of the tanks was all used up and the second tank was supposed to take over. It didn't. The engine stopped.

They began losing altitude. Then the engine roared again as gasoline from the second tank began to flow once more.

"Boy, were we glad," said Herndon.

And boy, was that an understatement!

body who had clout, obviously an admirer of Franco, and I was fired the next day, halfway through writing the afternoon programs. In the end, however, the firing proved to be a blessing. Henry Kaiser, the millionaire-industrialist, was living on the West Coast at that time and was one of the program's listeners. "He set the alarm for seven," Mrs. Kaiser once told me, "and if there wasn't any news, he'd go back to sleep after ordering everyone to buy Folgers Coffee." That's how I got to write news programs on the same network, but this time for six hundred and forty stations, rather than fifty. It was sponsored by Henry Kaiser.

***

But I want to tell you about that call from Stalin, which those who used to listen to the Frank Hemingway program will easily recall. On a morning when even yesterday's news was duller than usual, I arranged with a sound-effects man to have a telephone call interrupt Frank's reading of a news item involving the Soviet Union. It was an amusing bit of nonsense in which Frank was able to give the impression of a conversation between himself and Stalin. The Russian dictator, in Moscow, thought he had reached Ernest Hemingway, the well known author. When Frank said he was Frank Hemingway, Stalin retorted, "None of you Americans are frank. Your president wasn't frank with me at Yalta. But you should have heard what he said about Chiang Kai-Shek."

Stalin explained that he had just learned that all Americans have hobbies—they collect stamps, cocktail glasses stolen from taverns, replicas of locomotives, and hats of famous soldiers. He was going to show the Americans that they weren't the only ones who could be collectors. The Soviet Union had a five year plan, starting with borshch recipes from all over the world. He said Russians would get a good laugh from the way Americans make borshch, the creation of Russian peasants. After the sound- effects man's click that marked the end of the conversation, Frank said:

"Knock me down and call me a samovar, Joe Stalin wants a borshch recipe.

Anybody else want a borshch recipe?"

The response was remarkable. The sponsors were so pleased with the hundreds who wrote and asked for the recipes that I was surprised to find a fifty dollar increase in my weekly paycheck. There were, however, also hate letters from super-patriots that were not fun reading. "Only commi-lovers would put something of this sort on the air," wrote one from Seattle. But most who added comments to their request were pleased. One signed a letter Harold Posepian, Director of Yogurt-Borshch Peace Crusade, Inc. A letter from the University of Oregon campus in Eugene suggested withholding the recipes and using them as bargaining chips in the negotiations with the Soviet Union. Another from the same campus made the request for a recipe in Russian.

If, by the way, you want to try your hand at making Russian borshch, you can do it easily by making a rich beef soup that includes a can of sliced beets and the juice. About 15 minutes before it is ready for the table, add chopped up cabbage. Finally, add equal parts of lemon juice and sugar. About these, start with a quarter cup of each and keep adding to taste.

NOW A WORD FROM OUR SPONSOR

How to Get Yourself Fired

IN THE MIDDLE 1940's I was in charge of the KHJ radio newsroom in Hollywood from eleven p.m. to seven the next morning. The station was the West Coast outlet for more than fifty members of the Mutual Broadcasting Network from San Diego in California to Bellingham in Washington. My most important assignment was writing a fifteen minute early morning news program six days a week, which was sponsored three mornings by Folgers Coffee and the other three by a Los Angeles soap company. The announcer, with a unique talent for bringing to life the written words and imitating the voices of famous people, was Frank Hemingway.

Now, even though World War II was still raging and teletype machines were pounding away without a moment's pause all through the night, the "news" was usually yesterday's with the word "today" somewhere in the lead paragraph. One morning at about six-thirty, when Frank came in to read the script before going on air, he asked if there was anything new. I said, "No, godamit," and because I had a hangover I added, "I got a good mind some morning to write a script and tell the truth and you will read...'This is truthful Frank Hemingway for Folgers Coffee. There isn't any news this morning. Everything the teletype machines have been pounding out as though the Second Coming is at hand is yesterday's news with the word today thrown in.'"

I sure wouldn't blame you if you didn't believe me, but we did just that and got away with it for a

long time. I feel certain that there must still be quite
a few people on the West Coast who will remember
hearing Frank Hemingway every morning start out
in this manner: "Except for a development in London, where it's now three in the afternoon, everything in the news is again what you heard yesterday. But don't go back to sleep. I have to tell you
about an interesting telephone call I got from Joe
Stalin."

I got away with it for two reasons: I was in charge
of the newsroom and didn't have to ask anyone's
permission, and I knew that none of the executives
with power to fire me woke up that early. The program became a success because it was based on my
conviction that when people woke up and wanted
to know what happened during the night, and they
trusted the newscaster, they would go back to sleep,
and buy a lot of Folgers Coffee and the sponsor's
soap. Moreover, I often had Frank spice up a news
report with an entertaining comment. For instance,
when the news services reported that the United States
was supplying European nations with arms, but not
before extracting from them a promise that they would
not use them against each other, I had Frank comment: "This way of keeping Europe peaceful reminds
me of the old gentleman who kept bombarding his
friends with sermons about the evil of alcoholic beverages.
But to make sure they would read them, he always
wrapped the sermons around bottles of whiskey."

My "coup de grace"—the fatal blow—came when
the program became so popular it was put on the
air at four in the afternoon as well. My weekly sal-
ary jumped to $450 a week, equal to today's approximate
$1,250 or thereabouts. One afternoon the news wires

reported that the American representative to the United Nations had demanded sanctions against the fascist Franco administration in Spain because of human rights violations.

It was at that time a very controversial issue in this country, with Catholics strongly supporting the Franco regime. An unfavorable statement against Franco by a news commentator brought a flood of telephone calls to sponsors and station managers. I heroically stood by my First Amendment rights and wrote: "At the United Nations yesterday, the delegates decided that Franco of Spain is the number one "schlemiel" of Europe, and they picketed him with signs that read: Franco Unfair to the A F and L—All Forms of Liberty."

That did it. The word "schlemiel" (a nincompoop) sounded more sinister than the word "fascist" to somebody who had clout, obviously an admirer of Franco, and I was fired the next day, halfway through writing the afternoon programs. In the end, however, the firing proved to be a blessing. Henry Kaiser, the millionaire-industrialist, was living on the West Coast at that time and was one of the program's listeners. "He set the alarm for seven," Mrs. Kaiser once told me, "and if there wasn't any news, he'd go back to sleep after ordering everyone to buy Folgers Coffee." That's how I got to write news programs on the same network, but this time for six hundred and forty stations, rather than fifty. It was sponsored by Henry Kaiser.

***

But I want to tell you about that call from Stalin,

which those who used to listen to the Frank Hemingway program will easily recall. On a morning when even yesterday's news was duller than usual, I arranged with a sound-effects man to have a telephone call interrupt Frank's reading of a news item involving the Soviet Union. It was an amusing bit of nonsense in which Frank was able to give the impression of a conversation between himself and Stalin. The Russian dictator, in Moscow, thought he had reached Ernest Hemingway, the well known author. When Frank said he was Frank Hemingway, Stalin retorted, "None of you Americans are frank. Your president wasn't frank with me at Yalta. But you should have heard what he said about Chiang Kai-Shek."

Stalin explained that he had just learned that all Americans have hobbies—they collect stamps, cocktail glasses stolen from taverns, replicas of locomotives, and hats of famous soldiers. He was going to show the Americans that they weren't the only ones who could be collectors. The Soviet Union had a five year plan, starting with borshch recipes from all over the world. He said Russians would get a good laugh from the way Americans make borshch, the creation of Russian peasants. After the sound-effects man's click that marked the end of the conversation, Frank said:

"Knock me down and call me a samovar, Joe Stalin wants a borshch recipe.

Anybody else want a borshch recipe?"

The response was remarkable. The sponsors were so pleased with the hundreds who wrote and asked for the recipes that I was surprised to find a fifty dollar increase in my weekly paycheck. There were, however, also hate letters from super-patriots that were not fun reading. "Only commi-lovers would put something of this sort on the air," wrote one from Seattle. But most who added comments to their request were pleased. One signed a letter Harold Posepian, Director of Yogurt-Borshch Peace Crusade, Inc. A letter from the University of Oregon campus in Eugene suggested withholding the recipes and using them as bargaining chips in the negotiations with the Soviet Union. Another from the same campus made the request for a recipe in Russian.

If, by the way, you want to try your hand at making Russian borshch, you can do it easily by making a rich beef soup that includes a can of sliced beets and the juice. About 15 minutes before it is ready for the table, add chopped up cabbage. Finally, add equal parts of lemon juice and sugar. About these, start with a quarter cup of each and keep adding to taste.

GIVE ME BACK MY NEUROSIS

"Head Shrinking": It's a Living

I did not know that Art Hansl, a fellow copy editor on the Los Angeles Herald-Examiner, had a mental problem until the morning he failed to turn up for work on the copy desk. To the best of anyone's recollection, it had never happened before. He was always ahead of all of us, usually sitting in his chair and reading the Herald-Examiner's rival paper, the Los Angeles Times.

Around 9:30 a.m. that day, Agness Underwood, the city editor (in the 1960s Agness was still the nation's only woman city editor), came over to the copy desk and said the reporter, whose beat included the Los Angeles County General Hospital, telephoned the report that Art Hansl was in the hospital's mental ward. He was arrested for threatening those tenants in the apartment building, said the reporter, who were not Texans. "And," said Agness, pointing a finger in my direction, "he wants to talk to you. Take part of tomorrow off and find out what it's all about."

***

Art, who was shot and killed a year later by two rookie cops, was fifty-four years old at the time, powerfully built and handsome. He reminded me of Florian Bauer, the machinist who four decades earlier played a part in my becoming a journalist. Art was an introvert in every sense of the word, sitting silently beside me, editing copy and writing headlines which often

164

won prizes.

The Hearst-owned and operated Herald-Examiner, strongly unionized at that time, was able to boast the largest evening newspaper circulation in the nation. When the presses began roaring for the second of five daily editions at ten a.m. I took off to see Art in the mental ward of the County General Hospital. The ward was on an upper floor behind a locked door at the end of a bare corridor. In the door's center, about five feet from the floor, was a small square screened opening. When I pressed the button on the door's right side, and an attendant opened it, I saw that the corridor extended for about another twelve feet, then divided left and right to create a letter T.

To my surprise, I saw Art sitting in one of several chairs by the wall to my right. It was a noisy place with people talking, mostly to themselves. Some were walking around with their hands clasped behind their backs; others, also walking, were reading from their bibles, and there were those who sat in chairs staring into space, only their lips moving.

Another surprise came when I sat down beside Art. He began talking as though he was on his annual vacation and I had dropped in to see him. He wanted to know who had replaced him on the copy desk. Did I, as a member of the Newspaper Guild's negotiating committee, think there would be a strike this year? He asked that I buy a red necktie and give it to Lyle Abbott for his birthday and make sure that Lyle knew it was a birthday gift from him (Lyle was an oldtimer from the days when William Randolph Hearst rewarded employees more for their loyalty than their talent).

Suddenly I became aware of a change in his conversation. He was talking about my wife Helen in a more or less complimentary way, and several seconds passed before I realized he had also said, "I don't understand why you married a vegetable who thinks Freud is something you do with eggs."

Similarly, he praised Agness Underwood and suddenly I realized he had switched to something else. "...Don't worry, I'll sue them for a million bucks. The Chandlers (the owners and publishers of the Los Angeles Times) know damned well I've investigated them and know they are to blame for all the smog in Los Angeles. Everybody in Texas knows it."

Before leaving the hospital I learned that two psychiatrists would interview him. Then he would appear in a unit of the Los Angeles County Superior Court in the hospital to deal with mental patients, and the court would decide what would be done with him. In the meantime, a staff member of the hospital would be assigned to contact friends and relatives. The next day I was informed by telephone that Art, now fully aware of the problem he faced, wanted to avoid, if at all possible, a state institution.

He had adequate funds, something I already knew, but would need a guardian who would be responsible for him during his stay in a private sanatorium—if the court approved. I accepted the responsibility and was given the date of his appearance in Superior Court.

The hearing did not last long. The two psychiatrists testified that Art Hansl was a victim of paranoid-schizophrenia. Asked if that made him a dangerous person, both agreed that it was dangerous if an afflicted person drinks alcoholic beverages. The

judge turned to Art and asked if he drank, and I'll
be damned if Art didn't rise from his chair and said:
"Your honor, I often heed Timothy's injunction in
the New Testament, 'Drink no longer water, but use
a little wine for thy stomach's sake and thine other
infirmities.'"

About two hours later, a hospital staff member,
along with Art and me, were in the reception room
of a sanatorium at Compton in South Los Angeles.

A pretty young receptionist asked him to state his
name. Art replied, "Art Hansl, and your's?" The receptionist smiled at him and said: "You can call me
Gretchen." Art looked at me and winked: "Shall we
tell her about Hansel and Gretel in the Humperdink
opera?"

***

Compton is not far from downtown Los Angeles,
where the garish architectural monstrosity built by
William Randolph Hearst stands at the corner of 11th
and Broadway. I began to visit Art three, sometimes
four, times a week. The sanatorium was located in a
lovely small park. Before "We the People" figured
out a way to get rid of the Mexicans and latch onto
California in 1846, the property was part of a grant,
or "rancho," that belonged to a Mexican overlord.
Now it was a delightfully restful place for people
with mental problems. I always arrived around 3:30
with a copy of the latest edition of the Herald-Examiner and Art was always in the park waiting for
me. My visits, which began because of my commit-
ment as a guardian, soon became fascinating events.

He was amazingly well-informed on subjects ranging

from handicapping race horses to the backgrounds of the framers of the United States Constitution. The sanatorium's director, a Greek psychoanalyst, told me that Art Hansl knew more about ancient Greece than all the Greek professors in Athens. In retrospect, it seems to me that Art had fully recovered by the time I made my second visit. He glanced at the sensational stories on the front page of the Herald-Examiner and said, "God almighty. This is about sane people. I think you have to be crazy to consider yourself sane."

He grinned and added: "Et tu, Brute."

I learned a great deal about him during the more than two months he was in the sanatorium. He told me that he had been in and out of mental institutions during most of his adult life. He had a low opinion of psychoanalysts.

"They are businessmen above everything else," said Art vehemently.

"Get a list of them from the Medical Society and you'll find them always where the money is, in Beverly Hills, Encino, Malibu. Only occasionally is a dedicated soul found practicing in East Los Angeles or Watts. A prosecutor can find one who will testify that a defendant is this or that, and the defendant's attorney can find another, who may have a degree from the same university, who will testify his client is not this and that."

What I found most illuminating, however, was his revelation that most of the time he felt dull, insecure and almost tongue-tied. The only time he seemed to feel comfortable, said Art, was when he was in trouble, and he did not know how it happened.

"You know what I think, Bill," said Art, "I think

you can sell a short story to the New Yorker about a guy who keeps getting in trouble with his girl-friends, the boss, even the police. So they talk him into going to a psychiatrist. He sells his motorcycle, borrows money and spends it all on getting cured. When the psychiatrist tells him he is OK, that he is no longer a troublemaker, the girlfriends find him dull and uninteresting. You could call the article something like Give Me Back My Neurosis, or Happiness Is When You're In Trouble.

***

On the day before we got the report that Art was in the mental ward, Agness Underwood approached the copy desk with a page from a paper just off the press, and angrily demanded to know who had ed-ited the story by one of her favorite reporters. It seems the reporter had complained about the way his masterpiece was handled on the copy desk. We on the copy desk were being paid for editing copy, but that didn't stop Agness from unleashing a string of unprintable words at Art when he admitted that it was he had edited the story. Art, as I said, was an introvert. He sat listening quietly to the city editor's tirade. When it ended, he complained of a headache and went home. On the way home he brooded and kept thinking what he should have said while she upbraided him. He stopped to pick up two six- packs of beer and a pint of scotch. In his small second floor apartment he placed all but one can of the beer in the refrigerator and sat down in the chair from which he could see the sidewalk below and the bus-stop sign. He continued brooding and getting some comfort from a determination never again to let an idiotic woman tell HIM how to edit copy. He knew exactly what he would say to her tomorrow morning when he returned to work. He saw himself raising hell with Agness, and everyone applauding him.

Agness Underwood became more and more real. She was in the room and in a colloquy with him. No, she was not in the room. She was the woman on the sidewalk waiting for a bus. She had a gun. She was going to kill him. He staggered from the apartment and began knocking on doors. "A woman downstairs is going to kill me," he told startled tenants. "If you're not from Texas get the hell out of here. If you're not from Texas you can't help me."

***

When the Compton Sanatorium released Art he found himself without a job. George Hearst, the publisher, grandson of the "old man" who founded the Hearst dynasty, declared he would have no "dangerous crazy people" working for the paper. The Newspaper Guild's grievance committee, of which I was a member, tried hard to change his mind, but George was adamant, and we were compelled to drop the issue.

Art, however, was not jobless very long. He was soon working on the copy desk of the morning paper in Long Beach. Here, as everywhere else, he quickly established himself as a top-notch copy editor and headline writer.

And it is this very fact that got him in trouble and brought about his death.

When he called me to report that he was going to work on the Long Beach paper, I helped him find a home in nearby Seal Beach. It was in one of those structures so popular in California, a one-story rectangle building with three apartments on each long side and two on the shorter one. The front was flush with the sidewalk. Among the pots and pans I provided was a large two-pronged barbecue fork, which played a part in his death.

My own home at that time was a considerable distance from the ocean and Seal Beach, Studio City in the San Fernando Valley. But we kept in touch by telephone.

To better understand Art's tragic end, we have to know that in the early sixties, many, if not most, newspapers were still using linotype machines and galleys and similar paraphernalia in composing rooms to create newspaper pages for the presses. Dummies for each page indicated where the stories went, and a member of the copy desk staff was assigned the task of making certain that the news stories appeared where they were supposed to appear. The task often became tricky when deadlines were involved and lines had to be added to or trimmed from stories to fit allotted spaces without affecting the continuity of the stories. Art was particularly expert in that operation. He could glance at a proof, kill two inches of type and replace them with two quickly-written lines, without affecting the story.

One day he called me, I could tell by his voice that he was in trouble, and said that members of the staff stopped talking to him. He said that it began when auditors noticed that when he was assigned to the composing room the overall cost for putting the paper "to bed" was lower than when others were assigned to the same task. Management wanted to know why, and everyone seemed to have begun acting as though he was not there.

He firmly rejected my offer to come down and talk with some of the fellows, all of whom were members of the Newspaper Guild. And only two days later, at about six in the evening, he called again, and this time I could tell by the background noise that he was calling from a tavern. He said he had quit his job. He didn't even give them the usual notice. "I just walked in and said I'm through." I could not tell by the sound of his voice if he came to the tavern to drink or just to use the telephone, so I said I would come down and stay with him because tomorrow was my day off. He said it would take me at least two hours because of the heavy traffic, and for me not to worry about him. He was alright.

In the morning I got the news that he was dead. At the coroner's inquest, the two police officers who were cleared testified that they responded to a call from neighbors who complained that a drunken man kept pounding on their doors and demanding they leave California if they were not from Texas. The officers said they knocked on Art's door, identified themselves as police officers, and asked him to open up. "Are you from Texas?" Art demanded.

They said they weren't. All they wanted was to talk with him. He again refused to budge if they were not Texans. They testified that as they crashed through the door, he lunged at them with a large barbecue fork.

They shot him. It was a small local news item. The Herald-Examiner carried it, without mentioning that he once worked for the paper. It came to the attention of a Los Angeles Times columnist, who

GOD & ASSOCIATES, INC.

We Recycle Souls
(1-800-555-VISA)

LONG BEFORE TODAY'S PREACHERS—often trying to act more like Hollywood movie stars than holy men—learned to use the most sophisticated achievement of modern science—the color television set—to provide access to God, we had evangelists and cult leaders to keep our souls free from hell and perdition.

The acknowledged leader among those shepherds of this century's first two decades was Billy Sunday, whose real name was William Ashley. As a youngster, he wanted to be a professional baseball player, and actually became one for seven years, playing with Chicago, Pittsburgh, and Philadelphia. But he saw "the light" at the start of this century, and what a "light" it was. Billy Sunday's super-duper revival extravaganzas make today's color "come to Jesus" television programs seem like under-financed movies. Massed orchestras, huge choirs, and fire and brimstone attacks on sin and the devil, attracted thousands to his weekly revivals. He was an actor, no doubt about that. Facing his huge audience, he would roar a challenge at the unseen devil. "I will wrestle you, I will beat you, I will scratch you, I will bite you. And when I lose my teeth I will gum you to death. You hear me, devil?" He is reported to have delivered hundreds of thousands of converts. But whether this has made people act more kindly toward each other is anybody's guess.

Father "Peace It's Wonderful" Divine was among the more unusual members of this unique religious gentry. Before he turned up in New York in 1914, he was known as Major J. Devine in Georgia and elsewhere. He became "Divine" because Devine is a proper noun and divine an adjective, which brought him closer to God. When he died at the age of 88, his "Kingdom of Peace" consisted of 75 estates and hotels. He was a black man, but among the thousands who worshipped him were both black and white "angels," many of whom were sure he was God.

The requirements for becoming an "angel"f were quite simple—you traded all your worldly possessions for security in the hereafter in one of the many "heavens" he had created. The phrase "peace it's wonderful" became tied to Father Divine the way "let me make this perfectly clear" was to Richard Nixon.

Aimee Semple McPherson was an anomaly. She broke the Old Testament's clearly implied gender barrier the way Jackie Robinson broke baseball's color barrier. But it was not the fact that she broke into a field that always belonged to men that made her so unique. It was her sensational, flamboyant lifestyle and way of spreading the word of God. The newspapermen, I learned when I became one myself in Los Angeles, loved her because she was good for front page headlines at least four times a week. A substantial part of it was what we call today "hanky-panky" stuff.

***

Born on an Ontario farm in Canada in 1890 (she died at the age of 54), Aimee, at the age of 17, married a Pentecostal preacher named Robert Semple

and left with him for China. When he died a year
or so later, she and her newborn infant returned to
America, this time to the East Coast. Aimee completed the name by which she became known by
marrying a man named Harold McPherson, gave birth
to another child, ditched McPherson, left both children with their grandparents, and became a freelance,
roving evangelical preacher. For eight years she existed
"hand to mouth," by preaching the "old time religion"
to small groups of poverty-stricken people, providing
them, if not with bread, at least with spiritual comfort. "Believe in God.

He will never forsake you." "Trust in Jesus and
everything will come out right."

A few days before Christmas, 1918, Aimee arrived
at the City of Angeles in Southern California in a
beat-up old jalopy. Five years later, on New Year's
Day in 1923, thousands were on hand to witness
the consecration of her magnificent Angelus Temple
in downtown Los Angeles. She was a brilliant salesman. Her merchandise: Salvation, divine healing, baptism
by the Holy Spirit, and the Second Coming of Jesus.
There was always a good market for these items,
but nowhere was it as good as it was, and still is, in
Southern California, where a hundred spotlights light
up the sky to celebrate the opening of a new ham-
burger stand, and used car salesmen stand on their
heads atop elephants to draw attention to the reduced prices of their cars.

Aimee, loaded with spiritual qualities, was also a
woman of flesh and blood. What often happens to
people when they can say "I have everything" is
that their libido becomes over-active and they suddenly realize that they don't really have everything.

In this condition, Aimee gave in to the advances of a married man named Kenneth Ormiston, who was the engineer of the radio station from which her sermons were broadcast. They began to vanish mysteriously for days. On one occasion Aimee went swimming and could not be found for weeks. When she turned up, she declared that she was carried away by an angel and showed feathers to prove it. "Aimee, Aimee, Where art thou?" screamed the headlines. The bottom line, as we say today, is that Aimee Semple McPherson heeded not Matthew 26:41—"Watch and pray, that ye enter not into temptation; the spirit indeed is willing, but the flesh is not."

***

Let me now take you to the Pacific Northwest and a small city called Moscow in the northern part of Idaho. It was, and is, the home of the University of Idaho, and a half dozen or so miles to the west is Pullman, the home of Washington State University. Moscow had one of those small city newspapers, which used to get a sizable part of its income from printing wedding invitations, school and college graduation announcements, visiting cards, and business stationery. The paper concerned itself with local news and printing news releases from the university's top-notch agricultural department, for Moscow was in the heart of an exceptionally fertile valley.

Each day at noon, the telephone rang and a reporter wrote down the day's most important national and world news as it was being read slowly by someone in the Associated Press office in Spokane, a hundred miles to the north. Reporters in half a dozen small papers elsewhere in the region were doing the same. But both the newspaper and I play small roles in this saga.

The star is a druggist employee named Frank B. Robinson.

***

He was a handsome, likable, generous man—one of those unusual people who makes you feel you've known him for a long time. One night Frank B. Robinson had a dream. He dreamed that he was talking with God, and God told him He was accessible to each and every one of His children. Thus, he became the founder of a system which he called PSYCHIANA, by which, briefly, subscribers to a series of letters could learn how they too could learn how to talk with God.

He began by placing a small ad in a Detroit newspaper, and when the money began to roll in—mostly in quarters and dimes—he set aside fifty percent for ads in other newspapers. The business snowballed. The post office needed extra help, and Frank B. Robinson became thoroughly disliked in Moscow, especially by the clergy. The reason, I suspect, is that if you can talk to God yourself, you can dispense with ministers, rabbis and priests. In addition, Psychiana was not the sort of enterprise that expands the economy by creating profits and jobs for others. Indeed, the only business that benefited was the newspaper that printed the letters for the Robinson project. And the publisher, a dedicated defender of the "old time religion," made no secret of the way he felt about the blasphemous Robinson crusade. He began raising the price of printing the letters. And that's where events began that brought me front and center on stage.

Bill Marineau owned a small printing plant and published a weekly in a town east of Moscow. Occasionally, he came to Moscow to solicit printing jobs that did not require large equipment. He was passing the Psychiana business office when it occurred to him that Frank B. Robinson might have some work that the Moscow paper could not handle. When he learned the exorbitant prices Robinson paid the newspaper, he said: "If I had the proper equipment, I would print your letters for half the price you're paying and still have a juicy profit."

The upshot of this conversation was a decision by Robinson to buy printing equipment and start a new daily newspaper in Moscow to put the existing paper out of business. He went shopping for an editor, and when he came to see me in Wenatchee in his long black automobile, I was thrilled by the knowledge that he had selected me out of so many college-trained journalists. The new newspaper's full time United Press teletype wire service, its big city make-up and easily-read stories assured its success almost from the start. Frank B. Robinson was delighted. Doc, as I now called him, held himself completely aloof from the paper. When, however, something that particularly pleased him appeared in it he would drop into the office and casually begin to distribute twenty dollar bills to everyone.

Eventually, I began to have an uneasy feeling about Doc Robinson. I was troubled by the way he did things when I was with him. He always carried a big batch of twenty dollar bills in his pocket, using one or more to pay for each individual purchase or service, if it was a shoe shine or flowers from a hungry woman, he would hand them a twenty and say, "Keep it. God wants you to have it." All change went into another pocket, and when enough had accumulated he stopped at a bank and got more twenties.

Decades later, while researching Sigmund Freud, the same uneasy feeling surfaced in me when I began to see a similarity between my reason for wanting to become a trombone player in 1912 and his distribution of twenty dollar bills. Why did I want to become a trombone player? I was standing on the corner of Portage and Main in Winnipeg one day and saw a boys' band marching. They wore Scottish kilts and everybody on the sidewalks was yelling and applauding them. I envied them. I didn't care for the music, I just wanted to be one of them, and I wanted to be in the front line.

Trombone players are always in the front line. They can't play the trombone anywhere else while on parade, can they? Doc Robinson, I realized, got the same pleasant feeling of admiration from distributing twenty dollar bills as I did sitting on a platform playing "It Ain't Gonna Rain No More" on my slide trombone.

***

Few readers knew anything about Doc Robinson's ownership in the Daily News Review, which expanded its circulation among farmers because of its emphasis on agricultural news. It ultimately forced the other paper to close its doors,a nd is today known as The Idahonian. Doc Robinson added something new to his crusade. He began making periodic trips to Los

Angeles and other cities to lecture on ways to talk with God.

One day we were in his automobile on the way home from Spokane. I was sure that he knew I was not overjoyed with the business that made him richer and richer, so he apparently was not surprised when I said: "Doc, why in hell do you do it? Why do you take their money? You know you're fooling them."

He was silent for what seemed a long time, and finally said, "Bill, they get comfort from what I tell them. What difference does it make what I tell them? What would they have if I didn't tell them they can talk with God?"

And comfort it truly was. A week or so after our trip to Spokane, I had a chance to read a few of the letters from his "pupils." To the day I die, I shall not forget the contents in one of the envelopes. Postmarked from somewhere in Kansas, it contained a dime and a scribbled note: "The corn all dried up this year so this is all we got to send you. God Bless you."

I felt like crying and hated myself, Doc Robinson, and the First Amendment to the Constitution of the United States.

WHY DO JEWS "THUMB" DOWN JESUS

The Messiah Surplus

ONE THING I DON'T regret is that I won't be on hand to celebrate the Second Coming. I will by that time have taken, to use Hamlet's words, "the journey to the undiscovered land from whose bourne no traveler returns."

There is bound to be a great rush to buy Holy Bibles in order to refresh memories on what John the Baptist, Malachi, Daniel, Zachariah and many others, have prophesied would happen. There will be confusion and doubt, for I don't think there are two people in the whole wide world who have the same opinion of the way the Messiah will appear, what he will look like, and what he will say.

I can see the newspaper headlines now:

Washington Post SENATE TO PROBE MESSIAH'S CLAIM

Seattle P.I. SHAPE UP OR SHIP OUT; MESSIAH WARNS SINNERS

New York Times HE'S NOT "THE ONE," SAYS B'NAI B'RITH

National Enquirer MEDIA QUIZ MESSIAH ON "HAS H. GHOST A NAVEL"

I also feel secure in predicting that Jesus will be handcuffed and dragged off to jail if he talks the way the Bible says he did on his first appearance on earth. I base this on what happened to Upton Sinclair, the radical muckraking author, who nearly became governor of California after World War One, when the nation was in the grip of mass hysteria. Sinclair translated the Sermon on the Mount into modern

181

terminology and appeared on a street corner in Long Beach, California. When he began saying that meek people will someday inherit the earth, and lashed out at bankers, he sounded like a bolshevik agitator and was hauled off to jail.

***

Why did the Jews reject Jesus as the Messiah? Because messiahs were a shekel a dozen, and had been since the Jews lost their homeland and became wanderers. There was nothing in what Jesus said that hadn't been said, in one way or another, by the others. If you look carefully you may find lots of self-anointed messiahs still around.

Consider Sabbatai Zevi, acknowledged champion of false messiahs. He lived in the seventeenth century and had eighty thousand passionately loyal followers in Smyrna, Salonika, Alexandria, and Jerusalem who were convinced that he was the Messiah Jews were depending on to lead them back to their homeland. Then there was a disgusting, lecherous individual named Jacob Frank, in the eighteenth century, whose religious rites were often orgiastic, and who added himself to the Holy Trinity and made it a Foursome.

There were, as a matter of fact, enough phony messiahs for a yellow page section in the Holy Bible.

Jesus had the misfortune of being among Romans, who considered his preaching dangerous political agitation. So he was framed and executed.

There are, however, history students of that era, who believe that Jesus and the disciples were planning a rebellion against the Romans at the Last Supper, and that Judas, for thirty pieces of silver, betrayed them. They base this on the fact that nothing during the trial revealed anything that wasn't already known. Why should the Romans give Judas thirty pieces of silver if not for "classified" information?

Pieces of silver don't grow on fig trees, you know.

NAME! NAME! WHAT'S IN A NAME

When "Hymie" and "Abie" Spell Trouble

WHEN I AND MY two brothers and sister appeared at the Strathcona School in Winnipeg to tell somebody that we wanted to learn English and how to read and write, the principal, Mr. Sissler, took out a pad of paper from the desk drawer, lifted a pencil, and asked my older brother in German (which is almost the same as Yiddish):

"Vas iz zein naume?" (What is your name?), and my brother said, "Youdkeh."

"Nein," said Mr. Sissler, "JACK."

Then he pointed the pencil at me, and I said, "Shmeryl."

He shook his head and said, "WILLY."

My sister "Khaikeh" became "ANNIE" and my younger brother "Eeser" became "HARRY."

Mr. Sissler spoke several languages, as did many other principals of schools located in heavily populated immigrant areas. And changing difficult to pronounce foreign names to simple English Marys, Petes and Joes was quite prevalent. Neither we nor our parents were asked for permission to do that, but then we were "the huddled masses yearning to breathe free," and nobody was taking that freedom away from anyone in the United States or Canada, at least not at that time.

Changing names was not unusual in those days, especially among the Jewish population. And we had an excellent reason. Names like "Abie" and "Hymie" for children, in both Canada and the United States, assured future ridicule, abuse and a diminished opportunity for admission to some colleges and universities. So "Hymie" became Harry and "Abie" Albert.

Anyway, I doubt if I would be happier today if Mr. Sissler had changed Shmeryl" into "Sherman" and my sister "Khaikeh" into "Katherine." "What's in a name?" asks Shakespeare, "That which we call a rose by any name would smell as sweet." Not only was my father's name not Greene when he was born, it wasn't even Greenstein as the immigration people, and everyone who knew him, believed. It was "Mattice Kantorovich." Only in a czar's Russia could it happen. I am sure that were today's descendants of Jewish immigrants interested in the "roots" of their own families, many would discover that the way, and the reason, my father's name changed, was experienced by their own grandparents and great-grandparents.

***

Large families were the rule and not the exception, not only in Russia, but also everywhere else in the world. My own mother bore fourteen children, only seven of whom survived. The czars were not worried about large families. What they did worry about was having to dip into their own pockets to support large families when the breadwinner died. So the czars solved that problem with a law exempting from military service the oldest male of a family. The exemption cards, of course, bore no fingerprints or any other forms of identification beyond the holder's name. So eager were the czars to avoid digging into their own pockets, the card holders could go to Finland, Sweden, even America to work. The bottom

line was "send rubles to keep the home fires burning." These exemption cards played an important
part in getting many Jews out of Russia, who would
otherwise have been forced to serve in a tyrannical
czar's army. Here is how it worked: Card holder
Mordecai Abramovich reaches Finland or Sweden
or Montreal or New York. He buys a bible and with
a sharp knife or razor he carefully slits open the
bottom of one of the covers and slips in the card.
He addresses it to his friend Moshe Gimpel. Moshe
is seventeen and can't leave because males on reaching
fifteen must serve in the army before they can get away.

His own oldest brother, Abraham Gimpel, is already in New York. So Moshe Gimpel becomes Mordecai
Abramovich and leaves Russia.

My father's change from Mattice Kantorovich to
Mattus Greenstein came about differently. He did
not want to leave Russia, at least not at that time.
He had married my mother Miriam and was not eager to leave her to serve in the czar's army. It is
difficult to use the word "fortunately" in this case,
but the oldest son of a close friend named Isaac Greenstein
died, and Mattice Kantorovich became an oldest son
named Mattus Greenstein, in time to avoid army service.

***

The first member of the Greenstein family to leave
czarist Russia for Canada was my oldest brother Nehemia
Greenstein, who became Nathan Greene for reasons
that remain a mystery to me. Next to leave was my
brother Shmuel Greenstein. He needed no exemption cards of any sort because the czar's police were
at his heels for his political anti-czar activities. He

remained Shmuel Greenstein during his entire life. When I recall my brother Shmuel leaving without legal papers of any sort, I am reminded of my first wife Irene, who used to go fishing and come home with gunnysacks full of fish. I would say to her, "My God, don't you know there's a limit on the number of fish you can catch?" And she would become annoyed and say, "Of course I know there's a limit, but that's for people who have a license."

Then my father and brother Shlaimke left, my brother becoming Sam Greene and my father remaining Mattus Greenstein. Finally they had enough money to send for the rest of us.

Now we had a lot of problems. Youdkeh (Jack) had passed his fifteenth birthday. This we were able to settle with the help of a "macher," a man who knows how to slip a ruble into the hand of the right official, who then looks the other way. Then we bumped into something really serious, something few "machers" would even consider taking on. My grandmother was afflicted with the infectious eye disease called "trachoma." This meant the Canadian authorities would not let her enter the country. The "macher" sent off a telegram to Canada. The reply with instructions was prompt and told us to wait and they would find a Canadian "macher" who would go to Ottawa and set everything right. My mother was furious. She would not wait and she would not give an inch without our "bobbeh" (grandmother). She stomped around the room and shouted as though addressing a crowd: "What kind of a free country are we going to that they don't let an old lady in. A 'shwartzer yor' (a black year) should fall on the 'mumzeirim' (the bastards). God should send them the cholera.

We're going with my mother, and I will tell them what I think of them when we get there."

So off we went to America, I, my two brothers, my sister, my mother and grandmother. First to Kiev. I remember, so many, many years later, the huge railroad station, the long train ride, until we reached Kiel in Germany, then a ship that took us through a beautiful canal, until we reached Hull on the east coast of England.

We spent only one night in Hull, sleeping on thin mattresses spread out on the floor. Throughout the entire trip, from the time we left home until we arrived at our new home in Canada, which lasted more than three weeks, mother would not let us eat anything other than the food she had brought with her that was "kosher"—fried chicken parts, "kosher" slices of homemade bread, "kosher" pickles, tzimmes and cookies. Some of the people at Hull, however, ate food from a long table and we could see the steam rising from the dishes. On the large ship, which we took at Liverpool for the long trip to America, there were large barrels of boiled potatoes, which had not been peeled, and other barrels with salted herring. These mother allowed us to eat.

It was at Liverpool where the most unusual, rather frightening event occurred. We made the trip from Hull to Liverpool in a train that ran so fast that only when it stopped could we see houses and trees. When we arrived, a large number of wagons carried us and the large bundles of our possessions to a big boarding house where we had to stay until the boat arrived from America. The boarding house was quite a long distance from the ship. On the evening of the third day of our stay there, we were told that the wagons would come in the morning to haul us and our bundles to the big ship. Early morning found us outside the boarding house in groups, with bundles on the ground and children on top of them waiting for the wagons.

My mother and grandmother were standing nearby. I had just thrown away a banana, and I threw it away after peeling it and tasting it. Youdkeh said, "I think you have to eat the inside part." It was too late. Someone had stepped on it and squashed it. I was watching my mother. Suddenly, I saw her freeze. She stood there the way I imagined Lot's wife in the bible turned into a pillar of salt by God for looking back toward Sodom and Gomorrah. Then she began talking with our grandmother and gesticulating with her hands. We had not kept track of the days since we left our home in Russia, and she suddenly realized that this was the Sabbath, the day on which God rested and Jews were not allowed even to carry the Jewish bible to the Synagogue, let alone ride on wagons pulled by horses. It was a crisis of major proportions. They agonized over the matter and finally agreed to let our great baskets of "kosher" food and other family possessions be loaded alongside of us children on the wagons, and they began following the wagons on foot.

Suddenly the adults were horrified to find that they were following a different string of wagons. They had lost ours at one of the many turns while staring at all the marvelous sights en route to where the ship was docked. Both panicked, and this grew worse when they saw only gentiles, nobody with a beard and earlocks to indicate he was a Jew. They began asking everyone they saw, "Nah dalyeko Winnipeg?

Nah dalyeko Winnipeg?"

(How far Winnipeg? How far Winnipeg?) When someone finally got the message, and they again faced the dilemma of having to ride, my mother and grandmother held a conference and decided that, since the Good Book says it is alright to ride or even pull up water from a well in case of a crisis involving the saving of lives, then this was just such a crisis.

Meanwhile, at the dock, my sister, brothers and I sat on the top of our belongings, screaming for mother and grandmother, and refusing to let anybody touch anything. Oh, how wonderful, happy and welcome was the never- to-be-forgotten moment we saw them staggering toward us, each clutching an arm of an English policeman.

***

So, with God's help, as my father would say, we finally made it by ship to Montreal and from there by train to Winnipeg, where we all crowded into Nehemia's upstairs apartment until we could move into our own home. And in Nehemia's apartment I had my first frightening experience with Canadian technology. I had to go to the lavatory. The one I entered was nothing like any I had seen before, not at Hull and Liverpool in England, not on either of the two ships, and not on the train from Montreal to Winnipeg. I suspected what the odd-shaped white bowl on the floor with water in it was for, but there was a box on the wall near the ceiling to which a chain was attached. What could that be for? I gave the chain a jerk, and was immediately paralyzed with fear. There was a tremendous roar, and water began rushing into the bowl. In a moment it would become full and then the water would spill out on the floor. I fled, slamming the door after me, in the hope nobody would hear the loud sound the water was making. To my astonishment, nobody paid any attention. Mother was also startled when she first used the lavatory. When it was all explained to her, she shook her head and said, "Ah, Amerikeh Gunnif." I have never been able to find out the significance of this idiom. It means literally, "America, the thief."

But I had little trouble figuring out what was meant by "Only in America could it happen."

***

During our first winter in Canada, some six months after our arrival from Russia, father received a letter from Ottawa which informed him that the matter of our grandmother's trachoma had been resolved, and that he was at liberty to arrange for her departure from Russia. We had completely forgotten about her trachoma, for in Montreal they had not even bothered to ask if she had trachoma or any other ailments.

My 90th birthday finds only the four of us left. Youdkeh, Annie and Harry live in Winnipeg, I live in Washington. Youdkeh remains "Jack Green," without an "e".

***

In the "what's-in-a-name-department"—I was writing a headline reporting Zero Mostel's great stage performance portraying Tevye the Milkman in "Fiddler on the Roof." It was to be a "three-liner" to be spread over three columns. I wrote: "Zero No Zero in Fiddler."

I have always wondered, as I imagine others have, about the name Zero.

I assumed it was a pseudonym, but I have spent too many years writing not to have a feeling that there is a story somewhere in the name Zero, not a world-shaking one, but a story just the same. And my hunch was right. I heard it quite unexpectedly during a dinner party at the Los Angeles home of an actress friend, Evelyn Scott, at which one of the guests was a childhood friend of Zero's, another award-winning actor, Sam Jaffe. It's a very short story, but a delightful one. Mostel's real name was Sam, and his mother was (I don't like the adjective) a typical Jewish mother; that is, a mother who lives only to make certain that her children are well-fed and warm, and worry themselves into sickness if a child doesn't eat enough. "You don't want to die from consumption, do you? So don't eat like a bird."

But if you're mischievous, as Sam Mostel was, a Jewish mother can out- do Sara Bernhardt: "Why are you doing this to me? Why don't you just put a knife in my chest? A boy with a father whom everyone respects should want to bring a mother to tears?"

One day, said Sam Jaffe, Mrs. Mostel was particularly annoyed and shouted at her son: "You are a 'gornisht', you will always be a 'gornisht', and you will die a 'gornisht'." "Gornisht" is the Yiddish word for "nothing." "Nothing Mostel" for a name would sound silly; Sam Mostel believed "Zero" sounded better.

***

Let me conclude with a brief story about a scholarly Boston lady, who while visiting friends in New York, saw a lovely meticulously-dressed little girl and could not resist asking her, "What is your name, darling?"

"Shelly," replied the darling.

"How wonderful it is to be named after a poet," said the Boston visitor.

"Shelly Temple is a poet?" said the surprised darling. "I am Shelly Horowitz."

A DOG'S BEST FRIEND
IS A LONELY OLD MAN

End of A "Love Affair"

I GUESS I FIRST became aware that my small co-coa-colored dog Willy had become an integral part of my own existence around 1978, or perhaps it was in 1979.

The awareness came as a sort of spinoff from a slowly developing, and finally inescapable realization that my own future was practically all behind me; that I had turned eighty and was no longer able to overcome obstacles and cope with a world of electronics, chemicals, and gene- splitting technicians—a world where computers are even performing the functions nature had assigned to the human cerebrum.

I had become an anachronism, no doubt about that; I found that even my Last Will and Testament—prepared years earlier—was inadequate in this new world.

It was while I was trying to rewrite the last will and testament that an emotionally troublesome thought surfaced which had never occurred to me before—I needed to find a home for Willy—a home where Willy would be living without me.

Willy himself, by that time almost five, was on the floor a few feet from my typewriter, staring at me. No, I was not mistaken! Willy was staring reproachfully at me.

Finding a home where Willy might live comfortably without me became almost an obsession. I thought of my friends, all of whom loved Willy, but I kept finding reasons why the home of this one or that one was unsuitable.

I eliminated a friend who lived on a second floor

apartment on a fast traffic street, another had a home without a fenced yard, a third would be forced to leave Willy alone while she was away at work, a fourth might try to teach Willy idiotic tricks to entertain friends.

And what about food for Willy? I made the nourishing food that sustained him. Beef kidneys and liver cooked with onions and barley, and often an envelope of flavoring. And when we had need to be away from home, I always brought along Willy's food.

You see, the world changed only for me. It didn't change for Willy. I was his whole world, and it changed only when I was away from him for an hour or two.

I finally decided to rewrite my last will and testament with a provision that a codicil would be added as soon as I found a suitable home for Willy. And so the days and weeks and months passed. I continued finding homes for Willy along with explanations why they were not suitable.

You want to know something? Willy was an utterly pliant? pliable? member of the canine species. I did not even have to go through the customary practice of house-breaking him. He seemed to have discovered somehow what pleased me and what didn't. When I shook my head and said, "No Willy, no," he knew exactly what I meant. Surprisingly, he rarely barked, except occasionally when he heard other dogs bark.

I told a neighbor who asked me why he hardly ever heard Willy bark that it was probably a hangover from a former life when Willy was a police dog and was drafted by the CIA to work with agents on a sensitive assignment related to National Security.

***

It never occurred to me that I might survive Willy and have no need for a codicil to my last will and testament. It never occurred to me that there might come a day when I would have to take Willy to a veterinarian to remove from his throat something I believed he had swallowed and was having trouble dislodging by coughing, that fifteen minutes after walking into the pet clinic with Willy in my arms, I would be walking out numb with shock and knowing that his death was not in some distant future, it was around the corner. His heart had enlarged and was pressing against his windpipe. The coughing was a struggle for air.

Adding to my despair and bewilderment, the veterinarian informed me that the expanded heart also affected Willy's kidneys. Digitalis, a salt- free diet and diuretic tablets now keep Willy alive. I can figure on having Willy around for about nine months, perhaps even a year, said the veterinarian, but overexertion and any number of other unforeseen developments can take him at any hour.

***

"Willy does not feel pain the way people do," said the veterinarian.

"What he feels can best be described as discomfort."

That is what you learn from biology, physiology, neurology and the pictures and drawings and diplomas scattered over the walls of pet clinics.

But that does not describe Willy, and the way he reacts to my moods and eccentricities. It he doesn't feel pain, he knows that I do.

I am in my overstuffed chair watching television. Willy lies spread- eagled on the carpet. He stares at me unblinkingly, his glance shifting direction to keep me in focus when I reach for something or rise from the chair to go into the kitchen or bathroom. I laugh at something on the television screen and Willy's tail wags furiously. I change channels and listen to Luciano Pavarotti singing in Rigoletto. Willy straightens his forelegs to frame his head and rest his face on the carpet. He doesn't like opera.

Would you believe me if I told you that on long trips in my car, resting on the back seat, he knows that three clicks of the directional signal, a pause, and three more clicks means we're heading for a rest area?

No pause and we're only passing another vehicle. The pause brings him hurtling onto the front seat, quivering with excitement.

Well, Willy keeps staring unblinkingly, for not much has happened to trigger excitement since he went on medication. And as I stare back at him, it is clear to me that he is aware of the bleak, lonely days that will be mine when I awaken one morning and find only his lifeless body.

***

Willy lived on for another 14 months. Goodbye, little Willy, I shall never forget you.

MY LAST HURRAH

End of A Long Writing Career

I KNOW IT MAY come as a surprise, but I have to tell you that I have been racing against the clock for a long time while trying to make a written record—"before it is too late"—of events during my lifetime, in which I or members of my family participated—events, at least some of which, are pertinent to life in today's world. You see, in addition to the usual infirmities that afflict aging people, I made the distressing discovery some years ago that the cells of an artery feeding oxygen to the sensory part of my brain were dying at an ever-increasing rate and bringing closer and closer the end of my sixty-year writing career.

That is why I am naming this part of my life MY LAST HURRAH, for it is getting late for me, my friends, very, very late.

***

I first began to suspect that something was happening inside my head in the fall of 1973 while revising a few chapters of my Louise Bryant biography. I had signed a contract with Warren Beatty for its use in a movie six months earlier, and while working on the revisions, I was dreaming of a Brink's armored car pulling up in front of my home with a trunkful of money. Suddenly I became aware that I was doing something unusual unconsciously while typing. I was pausing occasionally to recall what I had written a couple of pages earlier, to assure continuity of narrative. It had never happened before. As a self-trained reporter, I learned to avoid none-filled pages. I usually needed only a few words to recall a complete scene—"thin eyebrows," "jittery" was all I needed for a description of a defendant on trial. I rarely came to an interview with a pad and pencil the way you see them on television, for this usually puts those you interview restlessly on guard. I wrote the story just about the way I would have told it to my wife when I returned home and she wanted to know what happened.

One day I told my first wife Irene that John C. Stevenson, a candidate for Washington State Governor in the Democratic primaries, had called his rival Clarence Martin a "big putz." She looked puzzled. From then on I made sure all my wives knew the Yiddish word for "penis."

***

Nine years passed before the movie "Reds" was released early in 1982.

A lawsuit in which Paramount Pictures and Warren Beatty were defendants, and I and my penultimate wife—that's the one next to the last—were plaintiffs, was settled out of court to everyone's satisfaction.

During most of the nine years I had little reason to talk with doctors or neurologists about what ultimately became for me a disastrous affliction. What, after all, is unusual about an old man being forgetful? As a matter of fact, I would like to forget that I voted for Lyndon Johnson and worked on a Hearst newspaper, for which I am sure I will be punished on Judgment Day.

I had a lot of spare time in those days, and to avoid boredom, I sometimes watched television when I could find something worth watching.

Thus, I discovered that President Jimmy Carter's wisdom, his talent for getting at the root of a thorny problem and coming up with a brilliant solution, had been greatly underestimated. I was juggling the channels in search of an interesting program when I bumped into a Jimmy Carter news conference. When I heard the word "abortion" I knew that it was my kind of a program. I seemed a reporter had brought up the question of federal funding of abortions for poor women. Since abortions had become legal, said the reporter, would not the government be practicing discrimination if it deprived poor women of such an important need, which is legally available to all rich women?

President Carter was silent for a few moments. Then came the "that's life for you" justification. "Poor women," said the President, "have always had to get along without many of the things rich women have."

You can't quarrel with that, can you? "That's life for you." If poor women can get along without Mercedes automobiles and thirty thousand dollar earrings, they can surely get along without the few minutes of pleasure sex provides, can't they? Precepts to live by—Sex is for the Rich / Make My Day / Read My Lips.

***

What finally prompted me to make a doctor's appointment was a growing feeling that my problem was not entirely due to my age. It seemed to me that another, a more important, element was involved. Mine was not the usual form of forgetfulness. From memory, I was able to bring to my conscious mind a mental picture of a person or object, but the names didn't always come with them. Somewhat similarly, the recollection of what I had read seemed to depend on how important the subject matter was. These problems seemed to become more and more troublesome when I completed work on the Louise Bryant manuscript revisions and turned to other writing projects; this more or less for the same reason I watched television—to banish boredom. The truth is, I really enjoyed writing. Correction. I enjoyed writing and was not bored, only when it didn't have to conform to traditionally acceptable subjects and style of presentation.

Let me tell you about a funny thing that happened when I was on the staff of the Hearst-owned and operated Los Angeles Herald-Express. On page one of the Sunday edition there always appeared an editorial by none other than the boss himself. One day I found myself editing it along with other copy for the Sunday edition. I made one simple correction in the editorial.

I don't remember what it was, but when I came to work on Monday it was made clear to me what would happen if I ever again corrected Hearst copy.

"Greene," said Bill Ryan, the news editor quite seriously, "when Mr. Hearst spells "shit" with two "t's", don't for the love of God try to change it."

***

Well, there were many things about which I could have written to keep busy, but the news from Hollywood was that Beatty continued organizing for a movie and one of his promises to me was that he would help get the Louise Bryant manuscript published. So I waited. And as I waited, I began to write about my little cocoa-colored dog Willy, who had become such an important part of my existence. I don't know of anything I ever wrote that gave me more pleasure than the story of Willy, who in a former life was a brilliant journalist.

I wrote at a leisurely pace, sometimes being away from my typewriter for a couple of weeks. I added paragraphs as appropriate thoughts surfaced.

I had begun without a title, but finally decided on THE PARABLE OF TOO MANY LOAVES because I found myself in a situation that paralleled the manner in which I lived today. Frustration began to become an element in my writing slowly, then as my condition continued to deteriorate with cells dying at a frightening geometric rate, there were times when frustration overwhelmed me and all I was able to do was sit and stare at poor little Willy in his overstuffed chair across from me.

But don't worry, Ma. If I don't keep trying I may become a cabbage, or worse, maybe a Vice President. You wouldn't want that to happen, would you, Ma? "Whatever happened to Bill Greene?" "He became a Vice President of the United States and nobody has heard from him ever since." Say hello to Papa for me, Ma.

I kept staring at Willy, and finally said, "Willy, is there a doctor in the house?"

The medical profession has certainly become specialized. When I was doing research in the San Francisco Bay area for the Louise Bryant manuscript, I found more midwives than doctors in the 1885 San Francisco city telephone directory. But leafing through the yellow pages of a telephone directory today, in any city, you will find so many classifications listed, it should come as no surprise if in a few years there should be individual listings for the nose, ear, and throat, with separate doctors for the right and left nostrils. On my first visit to an M.D., I learned that the cells of an artery feeling oxygen to the sensory part of the brain were dying. The result is that the rest of the brand does not immediately react to what the senses record. He said it was probably due to the artery hardening, or perhaps slowly contracting. He prescribed medication to expand the artery. It didn't work.

On a second visit some months later, he called the problem "intermittent cerebral ischemia." "Intermittent" and "cerebral" I knew.

"Ischemia," he explained, is a "suppression of the flow of blood." He said very little can be done because of my age. He added, to my distress, the information that the cells will continue dying at an increasing rate.

I felt the way defendants in criminal cases must feel on hearing a guilty verdict. "At the rate I'm going," I said, "I may soon become a babbling idiot." He comforted me by saying, "You will never be an idiot."

"I wouldn't bet on it, Doc," I said.

A year later a neurologist, after studying the x-rays, confirmed the M.D.'s diagnosis. He didn't, however, say the cells were dying. He said they were "atrophying." The bill I received suggests it costs more to atrophy than to die, as it will, I expect, if the undertaker calls himself a mortician.

***

If we set aside medical terminology, my understanding of what has happened, and what continues to happen is this:

When light rays reach your eyes and air waves your eardrums, that is, the sensory part of your brain, oxygen from your heart activates the rest of your brain, so that it instantly reacts. You can recall what you now see and hear by identifying them with your memories of similar objects or words.

A lack of oxygen from the heart plays hell with all that.

For instance, I am on the freeway. I want to get off on Grant Street, where I've never been. I see a sign: "Grant St. 1.5 ml's." The traffic is heavy. We drive slowly. Unless I keep repeating the words on the sign until I reach the offramp, I will do what I have done other times—forget to get off the ramp; recognize Mary Tyler Moore, my favorite actress, on television, but not her name; forget less than a minute after my car left the garage, if I pressed the gadget in the car to shut the electric door.

I am talking with you about a mutual friend. YOU: "I know he is a victim of schizophrenia, but he is so difficult to talk to."

"But you have to remember that schizophrenia often puts one in a new, self-created world, and you can hardly expect normal behavior from a victim of...(I have forgotten the word schizophrenia)."

An annoying result of the brain failing to react instantly to what I hear on radio or television is that the words seem to tumble over each other and are difficult to comprehend. It is odd, weird, crazy, bizarre. I can carry on a conversation, or be writing a letter or an essay, and suddenly find myself struggling to find even the simplest words to express what I have to say. Hell, I consider myself an expert on words, especially those infrequently used. "Uxorious" is an adjective applied to a husband who is so treacly attentive to his wife she feels like regurgitating each time he opens his mouth. A "sesquipedalianist" is a multi-syllabist who uses long words. "Mnemonics," mnemonics... let's see... mnemonics... oh, yes, it means the sort of things you do to help you remember to mail a letter. And long before I knew that H. L. Mencken had once called someone a "pediculous senator," I knew that "pedicule" was the Latin word for "louse."

***

Now it's all over. As I near my ninety-second birthday, it's all behind me, and I feel somewhat proud of myself. I will forget the frustration that often overwhelmed me. I know I will not win the Nobel prize for literature, but there are other possibilities.

Did you ever hear the story about the woman who brought her son to one of those clairvoyant women who foretell the future? "Tell me if he'll become a President or a millionaire or what?" the mother said. The crystal ball-gazer studied the son and said, "If he lives long enough he may become famous for his age."

Sure, there are a lot of people in their nineties who continue contributing to the welfare of humanity. But did any of them also have six wives and play trombone in treble clef? What counts, you have to agree, is that despite the obstacles and struggle to write, I achieved my goal.

***

I made it, Ma. I told you I wouldn't become a cabbage or a Vice President lost in the shuffle. It wasn't easy, Ma, but I made it. I did want to write another essay, Ma, but as the bible of the "goyim" says, "the spirit is willing, but the flesh is not."

It was going to be called: OLDSTERS BEWARE OF EUPHEMISMS.

A euphemism, Ma, is... well, remember those little houses outside of homes? When you put them inside homes and call them "rest rooms" or "his" and "hers", which sound nicer? All these nice-sounding names are called "euphemisms." You see, Ma, we all feel better if we read in the papers that "the new correctional institution will have X number of beds," than if we read "the new prison will have X number of cells." Willy is not a mongrel, he is a "mixed breed." I am not a tired, lonely old man, I am a "senior citizen" and with the help of God, I have reached my "golden years." I wouldn't wish such "golden years" on my worst enemy, Ma.

I would urge oldsters not to accept euphemisms in place of money for increased costs of medicare, and other sharp-shooting gimmicks. I would rally oldsters with a "shibboleth" the way it says in the Old Testament that Jephtha rallied his Gibeonites against the Ephraimites. I would have them shouting again and again SAY NO TO NO DOUGH... SAY NO TO NO DOUGH.

I would also proclaim an OLDSTER'S MANIFESTO: "Oldsters of the world unite. You have nothing to lose but your change to greedy free-enterprisers. Euphemisms are the opium to seduce you into feeling that all is well, when for millions, existence is hell." SAY NO TO NO DOUGH... from about and below... SAY NO TO NO DOUGH.

Well, Ma, that's it. It's getting late. "Dasvedan'ya." You remember your Russian, Ma, don't you? It's the Russian way of saying "Till we meet again." As agnostics, Ma, maybe we will.

E 169.1 .G73 A3 1991
Greene, William, 1897-1991.
Nine decades